# An Executive's Guide for Moving From U.S. GAAP to IFRS

# An Executive's Guide for Moving From U.S. GAAP to IFRS

Peter Walton

First published in 2009 by
Business Expert Press, LLC
222 East 46th Street, New York, NY 10017
www.businessexpertpress.com

ISBN-13: 978-1-60649-023-5 (paperback)
ISBN-10: 1-60649-023-0 (paperback)

ISBN-13: 978-1-60649-024-2 (e-book)
ISBN-10: 1-60649-024-9 (e-book)

DOI 10.4128/9781606490235

A publication in the Business Expert Press Financial Accounting
collection

Collection ISSN (print) forthcoming
Collection ISSN (electronic) forthcoming

Cover design by Artistic Group—Monroe, NY
Interior design by Scribe, Inc.

First edition: August 2009

10 9 8 7 6 5 4 3 2 1

Printed in the United States of America.

# Abstract

The book reviews different issues relating to the possibility that the Securities and Exchange Commission (SEC) may eventually mandate the use of International Financial Reporting Standards (IFRS) for use by listed companies and delegate to the International Accounting Standards Board (IASB) the task of providing accounting standards for the United States.

The first chapter reviews the international movement to converge on a single global basis of accounting for listed companies. It also discusses the experience of European companies, where 25 countries adopted IFRS in 2005. The second chapter analyzes the position in the United States. It looks at the advantages and disadvantages for corporations and explains the convergence program being followed by the Financial Accounting Standards Board (FASB) and the IASB. It also looks at the SEC's activities in this area and then sets out the challenges to be addressed by U.S. corporations if IFRS are adopted.

Canada has made the decision to switch in 2011, and the Canadian experience is discussed as offering a blueprint for the United States. This is followed by an extensive analysis of the technical differences between IFRS and U.S. Generally Accepted Accounting Principles (GAAP).

The last two chapters explain the organizational structure of the IASB and its standard-setting process, and then the evolution of the international standard-setter from its beginning in 1973.

# Keywords

Convergence, adoption of IFRS, global standard, International Financial Reporting Standards, U.S. GAAP, SEC requirements, International Accounting Standards Board

# Contents

# Acknowledgments

The content of the book was greatly influenced by Ian Hague, a principal at the Canadian Accounting Standards Board. I am very grateful to him for his help. I am also grateful to U.S. colleagues for advice, particularly Professor Gary Meek (Oklahoma State University), as well as Professor F. D. S. Choi (New York University) and Professor Mohammed Hussein (University of Connecticut).

The initiative for the book came from David Parker of Business Expert Press, and I am grateful to him and his team for their enthusiasm in moving from idea to finished product.

I should also like to thank the trustees of the International Accounting Standards Committee (IASC) Foundation for permission to cite from the International Financial Reporting Standards (IFRS) and related literature, as well as the Canadian Accounting Standards Board (AcSB) and the Canadian Institute of Chartered Accountants (CICA). Any changes to the original material are the sole responsibility of the author of this work and have not been reviewed or endorsed by the CICA.

# Disclaimer

Comment and analysis of a general nature, as given in this work, are not a substitute for dedicated professional advice relating to an entity's or an individual's particular circumstances. Users are cautioned to read this publication in conjunction with the actual text of the standards and implementation guidance issued and to consult their professional advisers before concluding on accounting treatments or other actions related to adoption of IFRS.

# CHAPTER 1

# The Worldwide Move to IFRS

Anyone who had not been keeping an eye open for international developments in financial reporting over the last 5 years would have been astonished to listen to Christopher Cox on August 27, 2008. On that day, the Securities and Exchange Commission (SEC) chairman announced that the regulator was to set out a roadmap that could result in U.S. companies using International Generally Accepted Accounting Principles (GAAP) from 2014 onward.

If you did not know that Canada had decided in 2006 to switch to International GAAP in 2011, and Japan, Brazil, China, South Korea, and India were doing the same, you could well ask, how could that happen? The answer, in headline terms, is that it is a combination of two strands. Principally, since the 1960s, business has become more and more global and has lost a significant part of its national identity. Once you have global players reporting to global finance markets, it makes sense to have global financial reporting rules.

The other strand is some loss of confidence in GAAP. This was part of the fallout from the Enron crash: before then U.S. regulators thought, with some justification, that U.S. GAAP were the best, most rigorous accounting standards in the world. Enron and others demonstrated that even U.S. standards could be manipulated dramatically.

The standards Cox was talking about are known generically as International Financial Reporting Standards (IFRS). They go back to the beginning of the 1970s when partners in what are now Deloitte and PricewaterhouseCoopers observed that businesses were making more and more international transactions. They thought this called for a common understanding of how the transactions should be measured. They brought together the American Institute of Certified Public Accountants

(AICPA) and professional accounting bodies from eight other countries to create a voluntary body to write what, at the time, they called International Accounting Standards (IAS).

A collection of standards was built over the following decades, primarily influenced by the Anglo-American approach to financial reporting. As these standards increased, they were used by many national standard-setters as a model for their own national standards. A key development started in 1987 when the International Organization of Securities Commissions (IOSCO) agreed to work with the international standard-setter to develop rules for international listings.

The SEC is a founding member of IOSCO, which brings together securities regulators from all the major capital markets. At that time each market had its own rules, and companies that were listed on several national exchanges had to follow different accounting and other requirements in many of them. IOSCO had the idea of creating a listing "passport." Companies would report according to the listing requirements of their home or primary exchange as usual. But if they wanted to be listed elsewhere, all the exchanges where they had a secondary listing would ask them to meet the same set of IOSCO requirements and not national rules.

There followed 10 years and more detailed work on extending and improving the IAS. The year 2000 was the next turning point. The professional accounting bodies that had supported the standard-setter for nearly 30 years agreed that it was to be reconstituted as a stand-alone, private body like the Financial Accounting Standards Board (FASB). Its standards would be written by a small group of technical experts. IOSCO voted to accept the standards as the basis of reporting where a company had a secondary listing. This new beginning was immediately given a further boost by the European Commission, the executive arm of the European Union (EU). The European Commission announced that it was to require all European, listed companies to use IAS from 2005 onward.

The reconstituted standard-setter, the International Accounting Standards Board (IASB), came into existence in 2001. As it turns out, it was surfing along the crest of a wave that was to reach many countries in a dramatically short time. In Europe, countries that are not part of the EU such as Switzerland had already been using international standards voluntarily for listed companies, while others such as Norway decided to switch to maintain comparability with the rest of Europe. Australia and South Africa decided to adopt IFRS in 2005 as well, with New Zealand making adoption voluntary in 2005 but compulsory from 2007 onward.

As Christopher Cox noted on August 27, "Today, more than 100 countries around the world, including all of Europe, currently require or permit IFRS reporting. Approximately 85 of those countries require IFRS reporting for all domestic listed companies."

The next key date for IFRS will be 2011. That year should see Canada, Brazil, Japan, China, Korea, and India move to the international standard. Under the SEC roadmap, 2011 is the year when the SEC should decide finally whether the United States should also move to IFRS, with a staggered transition possibly taking effect in 2014.

## How Do IFRS Compare With GAAP?

Curiously, the FASB and the international standard-setter came into existence in the same year—1973. Their standards are also very similar insofar as they are both within the body of what is known as Anglo-Saxon accounting and they have many common influences. Both standard-setters use virtually the same conceptual framework, and they are currently revising their respective literature to have a single, common framework.

Most financial reporting regimens used in developed countries can be classified as coming from one of two traditions. The Code Law, or Continental European tradition, traces its roots back to the 17th century. Accounting rules in this tradition are typically found in statute law and a national Commercial Code, and they are administered by the state. They are closely related to measurement of profit for taxation.

The Anglo-Saxon tradition dates from the 19th century and is the product of the Industrial Revolution. It has evolved as part of the mechanism whereby investors share risks by participating in the financing of large companies. Anglo-Saxon accounting is about communicating to investors. Although now we are used to having independent standard-setting bodies such as the FASB, over most of the last two centuries the rules of Anglo-Saxon accounting were worked out in detail by accounting professional bodies such as the AICPA.

This brings us to another significant common influence: the big auditing firms. When accounting standards were set by accounting professional bodies, many of the people who sat on the standards committees were actually partners in larger audit firms. Since the 1950s, the audit business has undergone a series of waves of international expansion and consolidation through mergers. We now only have four very big international firms, although there are other significant but smaller international networks.

The creation of today's big international firms started when American and British audit firms began to follow their growing corporate clients into other countries in order to maintain their service. From the 1950s onward, there was a series of mergers between American and British networks. For example, Coopers & Lybrand—now part of PricewaterhouseCoopers—first got together in 1957 through an agreement between Cooper Bros. in the United Kingdom and Lybrand, Ross Bros., and Montgomery in the United States. These firms have dominated the international audit industry ever since. Through their own internal exchanges of staff and techniques, and by servicing national standard-setting committees, they have ensured that the national variants of Anglo-Saxon accounting have not deviated too far from each other, even if one can point to many differences at a detailed level.

While IFRS and GAAP come from the Anglo-Saxon tradition, there is one thing that sets the United States, and GAAP, apart from other Anglophone countries: the litigious environment of the United States. IFRS, by their very nature, must be written to work independently of any national legal system. U.S. standards, on the other hand, have been written for many years with many detailed rules. These enable companies and their auditors, when faced with a claim, to point to a rule book and say to a judge, "We followed the rules—so we have no case to answer." IFRS are more generic in nature and call for professional judgment to apply them to particular cases. In many cases, the company has to decide which standard applies in their circumstances, and subsequently that judgment could be more easily challenged in the courts. IFRS are written at a more generic level and have very few industry-specific rules.

Up until Enron, people in the United States were pretty happy with GAAP. Since Enron, some have felt that very detailed accounting standards make it too easy to manipulate data to get the results you want.

The Sarbanes-Oxley Act mandated an SEC study of principles-based standards. This study argued that

> rules-based standards can provide a roadmap to avoidance of the accounting objectives inherent in the standards. Internal inconsistencies, exceptions and bright-line tests reward those willing to engineer their way around the intent of standards.[1]

The study recommended that the United States should move to an "objectives-based" approach to standard setting. It suggested that accounting standards should state the objective the standard was trying to achieve and then give detailed guidance as to how one achieves that objective. However, the corporate preparer could not rely on simply complying with the guidelines as a means for meeting the objective. Both preparer and auditor would have to use their judgment as to whether the objective had been met. The SEC study commented that it was understandable to have bright-line rules but that such rules could often result in the accounting failing to represent the economic reality. The costs were therefore higher than the benefits.

In this context, you can see that a move to a set of standards with the same intellectual origins but different legal frameworks might appear a lot more interesting to U.S. regulators. David Tweedie, chairman of the IASB, testified in Congress before the Subcommittee on Commerce, Trade, and Consumer Protection of the House Energy and Commerce Committee in February 2002. He said,

> US accounting standards are detailed and specific because the FASB's constituents have asked for detailed and specific standards. Companies want detailed guidance because those details eliminate uncertainties about how transactions should be structured. The IASB has concluded that a body of detailed guidance (sometimes referred to as bright lines) encourages a rule-book mentality of "where does it say I can't do this?" . . . Our approach requires both the company and its auditor to take a step back and consider whether the accounting suggested is consistent with the underlying principle.[2]

The SEC study did not in fact think that IFRS could be described as principles-based standards, nor do IASB members assert that all their standards are principles-based. However, the IFRS do structure the standards to identify principles, and they do not usually give very detailed application guidance.

## Why Use IFRS?

For the United States, clearly one reason to move to IFRS would be to move away from rules-based standards. Another reason would be that since 2008 foreign companies registered with the SEC and using IFRS can list their securities in the United States without reconciling with GAAP.

However, outside of the United States, the main reason cited for adopting IFRS is that of comparability. If all companies reported using IFRS, then it becomes much easier for investors to compare globally. In general, it is an advantage claimed for international harmonization; without it, investors are limited to their national market. Without IFRS, comparisons are limited and inefficient companies are enabled to survive because their performance cannot be compared to efficient companies that report under different rules. Comparability should therefore make for greater transparency and greater efficiency.

Some people may think that all financial reporting rules would measure profit and net assets in the same way. At a broad level, they do. Also, within the subset of Anglo-Saxon accounting there is a high level of common thinking. Even so, just a small difference in rules can impact earnings and equity. Prior to its adoption of IFRS, the United Kingdom used a quite different approach to deferred tax than was used in GAAP. This would sometimes throw up substantial differences for UK companies that reconciled their UK earnings and equity to GAAP for SEC purposes. If everyone is using the same rules, then the movement from one year to another is comparable, and the annual earnings should be comparable, although there is still the effect of management judgment on amortization, depreciation, and provisions.

An argument in favor of global rules put forward by stock exchanges is that investors want as wide a choice as possible, and using internationally acceptable reporting rules makes it easier for foreign companies to list on any exchange. Big international investors will locate their fund management in places where they have the easiest access to the widest range of businesses. Equally, U.S. companies using IFRS would find it easier to list outside the United States even if GAAP reports are widely accepted by foreign exchanges. Investors charge a discount for uncertainty if they do not feel fully confident that they understand the rules.

There is also an internal cost gain for multinational companies, as Peggy Smyth, vice president and controller of United Technologies, noted at a meeting of the International Financial Reporting Interpretations Committee (IFRIC) in 2008. She said that her company was already working on the transition to IFRS; 60% of its sales were internationally driven. They had many subsidiaries using IFRS in their national accounts, and it made sense to use IFRS for the whole group and not have to convert.

## The European Experience

The EU was the first major adopter of IFRS. The EU at the time consisted of 25 countries (now 27), including all the largest economies in Europe: Germany, France, Italy, and the United Kingdom. There are approximately 8,000 European companies listed on stock exchanges within the EU. The European Commission decided in 2000 that these companies should switch to IFRS in 2005. The official statute that mandated this was voted on in 2002: the IAS Regulation (2002/1606). This regulation automatically overrides national laws. While the changeover date was 2005, companies had to provide one year of comparative figures. Therefore, they had to be able to record sufficient information to prepare 2004 financials according to both national GAAP and IFRS.

The SEC roadmap envisages a possible switch in 2014, with the decision taken in 2011. This means that U.S. corporations would need to implement IFRS adoption plans very soon after the 2011 decision is made, as they would have to provide previous years' comparatives. U.S. companies normally have to provide 2 years of comparatives (i.e., they would need 2012 figures under IFRS); although European companies that are registered with the SEC were allowed to give only one year of comparatives when they switched in 2005, the SEC has no plans to relax the requirements for U.S. companies. European companies were required to publish 2004 financials using national GAAP, and then sometime before publishing their first 2005 financials, they had to give a 2004 reconciliation. This reconciliation compared the 2004 national GAAP figures with the 2004 IFRS figures. U.S. companies switching in 2014 would probably have to provide this reconciliation for 2012 and maybe 2013.

The Committee of European Securities Regulators (CESR) is the nearest thing to an EU-wide stock exchange regulator. The CESR coordinates the activities of individual national regulators. It recommended that companies should disclose in their 2003 financial reports their state of progress in preparing for conversion and what major differences they had identified.

The United Kingdom and Ireland are the only two EU member states whose national GAAP is part of the Anglo-Saxon accounting tradition, and therefore generically close to GAAP. In this section, examples are drawn from the UK experience as being more relevant to the United States than, say, the German or French experience, where there is a Commercial Code tradition and a strong link to taxation. The transition to IFRS posed quite different problems to them than to the United Kingdom and Ireland.

Aisbitt and Walton examined the 2003 disclosures of the companies making up the main UK stock exchange index, the FTSE 100. The researchers found 97 usable reports, which they analyzed on the basis of quality of the information. Their findings are shown in Table 1.1.

They defined the categories as follows:

- *Perfunctory*. The transition is mentioned but the report gave no indication of which recognition and measurement issues were likely to affect the company.
- *Adequate*. Individual recognition and measurement issues were identified.

**Table 1.1. 2003 Reports**

| Quality | Number |
|---|---|
| Perfunctory | 26 |
| Adequate | 34 |
| Detailed | 21 |
| Subtotal | 81 |
| No mention | 16 |
| **Total** | 97 |

- *Detailed.* Individual issues were identified and problems and possible impacts were discussed (usually with some quantification of these).

The researchers thought that this might be an indication of the preparedness of individual companies:

> We take the view that having the confidence to identify publicly the recognition and measurement issues is a reasonable surrogate for state of readiness. We would therefore suggest that all those that fell into the adequate or detailed categories gave evidence of having the matter in hand, whereas for the others it is open to question as to how advanced their preparations are.[3]

One could draw from this that about half the FTSE 100 companies were not very advanced in their preparations in 2003, despite the fact that they would still have to measure the 2004 result in IFRS. U.S. companies should bear in mind that analysts are likely to want information about possible impacts well before the transition period starts.

The same paper provided a table of the issues most frequently raised as a concern by companies (see Table 1.2).

**Table 1.2. 2003 Disclosures**

| Accounting issue | Number of companies | % of companies examined with disclosures re IFRS |
|---|---|---|
| Financial instruments | 43 | 53 |
| Pensions | 35 | 43 |
| Share-based payment | 30 | 37 |
| Deferred tax | 26 | 32 |
| Goodwill | 25 | 31 |
| Hedge accounting | 21 | 26 |
| Employee benefits | 17 | 21 |
| Intangible assets | 16 | 20 |
| Presentation and disclosure | 11 | 14 |
| Leasing | 11 | 14 |
| Impairment | 10 | 12 |

The fact that companies had to disclose their 2004 figures according to local GAAP and IFRS provided a useful opportunity to measure the differences that they actually recorded. Aisbitt identified the following impact on equity on a sample from which eight companies had been excluded (see Table 1.3).

In Table 1.3, it can be seen that there is no clear pattern in the way the transition affected large UK corporations. Further analysis in the paper shows that the main negative impact on equity was an increase in retirement benefit obligations, and the main positive impact was in property, plant, and equipment. However, most companies had small adjustments to a number of different line items.

The EU commissioned a report[4] on the impact of IFRS adoption. The report, prepared by the Institute of Chartered Accountants in England and Wales (ICAEW), was published in October 2007.

Some of its findings are as follows:

- There was widespread agreement that IFRS has made financial statements easier to compare across countries, across competitors within the same industry sector, and across industry sectors.

**Table 1.3. Equity Under IFRS**

|  | Equity increased | Equity decreased |
|---|---|---|
| Industry | No | No |
| Basic materials | 2 | 5 |
| Consumer goods | 9 | 2 |
| Consumer services | 8 | 17 |
| Financials | 9 | 11 |
| Health care | — | 3 |
| Industrials | 5 | 7 |
| Oil and gas | 1 | 1 |
| Technology | 1 | — |
| Telecommunications | 1 | 3 |
| Utilities | 1 | 6 |
| **Total** | 37 | 55 |

Source: Adapted from Aisbitt (2006), Table 1, p. 122.

- Sixty-three percent of investors thought that IFRS had improved the quality of consolidated financial statements against 24% who thought that IFRS had made it worse. The corresponding figures for preparers were 60% and 14%, respectively, and for auditors 80% and 8%.
- In many jurisdictions the increased amount of judgment required by IFRS as a generally principles-based set of standards presented considerable challenges, and some concerns were expressed about consistency of application.
- While there was a fair degree of satisfaction with the current suite of IFRS, certain standards were singled out for criticism, including IAS 39 *Financial Instruments: Recognition and Measurement*. A number of participants queried whether the valuations of intangibles required under IFRS 3 *Business Combinations* merited the associated costs.
- Based on the results of our online survey and application of the EU Common Methodology, insofar as this was practicable, the following is a broad estimate of the typical cost of preparing the first IFRS consolidated financial statements of publicly traded companies:

  - Companies with turnover below €500 million (0.31% of turnover)
  - Companies with turnover from €500 million to €5,000 million (0.05% of turnover)
  - Companies with turnover above €5,000 million (0.05% of turnover)

There is a growing body of academic research that studies whether the use of IFRS was "value relevant" (i.e., it changed the share price) and whether it reduced the cost of capital.[5] The ICAEW report summarizes the literature as follows:

The early findings suggest that IFRS financial statements include information that was not available under national GAAP and that investors use this information. IFRS has affected the value of companies, but the effect is not equally distributed.[6]

It is not clear that this has any implications for U.S. companies. For the share price to be affected, the market has to find more relevant information under the new system as opposed to the old. Because IFRS are more rigorous than national GAAP across the EU, or are more oriented toward investor needs, it is not surprising that share prices would respond. One could also expect that analysts and investors would have little experience using IFRS and so might take some time to adapt.

However, there are number of significant differences in the U.S. case. First, the IASB has been working on convergence with the FASB and has had a formal program in place since 2002 (more details will follow in chapter 2), so there has been and continues to be a positive effort to eliminating differences in the standards. Second, it is also debatable that the market would react significantly to areas where there *are* differences (these are discussed in chapter 4) since the differences may not be material for investors' decision purposes. Third, analysts already have a great deal of experience working with IFRS and by 2011 will have acquired more.

In March 2007 the SEC held a roundtable to discuss whether a reconciliation to GAAP was necessary for foreign registrants using IFRS. The participants in the roundtable were people active in U.S. capital markets. John White, director of the Division of Corporate Finance at the SEC, analyzed the discussions in a speech later that month.[7] He reported that the investor panel had said they did not use the reconciliation because

> many foreign private issuers report their year-end results and base financial reports in their home countries significantly in advance of when they file their Form 20-F's . . . for large institutional investors and analysts, this fact results in those parties going to the foreign private issuer's home markets for their information, and using IFRS to make their investment decisions. Credit rating agencies may do similarly.

He added,

> I was struck by how consistently the investor panelists told us they were not really using the reconciliation and in some sense preferred IFRS to U.S. GAAP. They pointed out that for many

industries and peer groups, IFRS is the most common accounting standard and so in order to understand that industry or sector, analysts must know IFRS and in fact, institutional investors
sometimes "reconcile" U.S. GAAP financial statements to IFRS in
order to make their comparisons and investment decisions.

## Supporting Infrastructure

The fact that Europe has been using IFRS since 2004 means, curiously
enough, that there is already considerable experience with the standards
within the U.S. financial reporting infrastructure. A number of foreign registrants were using IFRS voluntarily before 2004: a number of EU member
states allowed this when companies were listed on a foreign exchange, and
many Swiss companies such as Nestlé or Roche have also used IFRS for
some years. As a consequence, both the SEC and the major audit firms
already have a wide involvement with companies that use IFRS and have
been making inputs to the evolution of the standards for years.

It was actually the SEC, as a driving force in IOSCO, that suggested
to the IASB's predecessor body in the 1980s that the international bodies should work together. When the new structure was created (details
are in chapter 6), the SEC took a role as an official observer both at
the Standards Advisory Council (SAC) and the IFRIC. Currently, the
SEC has a deputy chief accountant, Julie Erhardt, responsible for liaison with the IASB.

Foreign companies have been filing with the SEC using IFRS for some
years, and since 2005 there are as many as 600 companies that file using
the international standards. This means that the SEC staff already has considerable experience working with IFRS-based financial statements. They
have also provided considerable feedback both to individual companies and
to the IASB and its staff through published reports and statements.

The major audit firms have been deeply involved with international standards from the very start. Since the creation of the full-time
professional standard-setter in 2001, the Big Four audit firms (KPMG,
Deloitte, Ernst & Young, and PricewaterhouseCoopers) have organized
themselves specially to deal with IFRS.[8] Typically, each national firm
within the network has a desk that deals with IFRS matters, and this
liaises with a global IFRS desk, usually based in London. National firms

send staff to the global IFRS desk for training and orientation. Technical queries are passed from the national office to the global IFRS desk to try to ensure a consistent application of IFRS throughout the world. The global IFRS desks also liaise informally with each other.

Of course, the Big Four maintain a close liaison with the IASB members and staff, participate in the deliberations of the IFRIC, and are represented on the (SAC). The IASB staff frequently discusses work in progress with the global IFRS desks and, in particular, asks for their help informally in carrying out fatal flaw reviews. The Big Four often send in implementation queries to the IFRIC. When the IASB sends out a discussion paper or exposure draft for comment, the Big Four try to coordinate the responses of national IFRS teams so that there is a single response from each firm.

The next tier of international networks—such as BDO, Grant Thornton, and Mazars—do, of course, have their own IFRS liaison structure, but the costs and benefits are different. The Big Four audit nearly all the world's multinational companies and can amortize the liaison costs more widely. However, as IFRS come to be used more widely for unlisted and smaller, listed companies, the larger firms outside the Big Four are likely to adapt their structures further.

The Big Four enjoy a close relationship with the IASB. Each one subsidizes the standard-setter to the tune of $2 million a year and invests a great deal in liaising with it. Against that, they audit about 10,000 multinationals across the world that use IFRS and have gained a great deal of experience in applying the standards. They publish detailed manuals and briefing literature.

## Conclusion

IFRS have been built up steadily since 1973. They have the same intellectual foundations as U.S. GAAP, and there has been a formal convergence program with the FASB in place since 2002. IFRS are endorsed by the IOSCO for use as a global financial reporting standard. They have also been the financial reporting rules for all listed companies in Europe since 2005 as well as a number of other countries. Japan, Canada, Brazil, India, and China are planning to transition to these standards in 2011. They are oriented toward reporting to investors but have far fewer bright-line rules than U.S. GAAP. Their application calls for judgments by companies and their auditors.

The main benefit of using IFRS is that it permits investors to compare the performance of companies that have their headquarters in different countries. In principle, it means that investment can be more effective and seek out the best returns globally. For companies it may well mean a lower cost of capital since investors have less uncertainty. Using IFRS makes it easier and cheaper for multinationals to list on foreign stock exchanges so they can attract a wider range of investors. It also helps stock exchanges since they can offer investors a wider choice. Multinational companies also benefit because many of their subsidiaries use IFRS and there is no need to restate for consolidation purposes.

Adoption of IFRS by EU-listed companies in 2005 provides a number of pointers to what the U.S. experience might be like should the SEC decide in 2011 to mandate a switch in 2014. In Europe, companies were slow to gear up for the switch, although investors wanted information well ahead of the switch taking place. The switch involves running parallel systems ahead of the deadline so that comparatives can be provided for the switch year. The impact on UK companies, where the national rules are not very different, was varied. Across Europe investors found that moving to IFRS gave enhanced comparability.

The SEC has been involved to an extent with the development of IFRS and since 2001 has sent observers to key committees. It has also worked with a significant number of foreign registrants that use IFRS. As a consequence, the staff already has considerable experience with this financial reporting base. The Big Four audit networks have significantly changed their internal structures to have a global center for IFRS that liaises closely with the IASB and provides training and experience for staff from national offices. There is already an important global infrastructure for supporting companies using IFRS, which number more than 10,000 across the world.

# CHAPTER 2

# Moving From U.S. GAAP to IFRS

This chapter looks at issues surrounding the move from U.S. GAAP to IFRS. We will look at the pros and cons of moving to IFRS, the convergence of standards between U.S. GAAP and IFRS, the role of the SEC, and the role of the FASB. From the perspective of a U.S. corporation, we will look at the costs, the benefits, and the challenges to be overcome. We will discuss a blueprint for action. Recognition and measurement differences are examined in chapter 4.

## Why Should the United States Change?

As early as 1988,[1] the SEC has supported the establishment of mutually acceptable international accounting standards. It subsequently has pointed out that "preparing more than one set of financial statements to comply with differing jurisdictional accounting requirements increased compliance costs and created inefficiencies."[2]

The 2007 Concept Release set out the SEC's ideas on (a) removing the 20-F reconciliation requirement for foreign issuers using IFRS (which it did later that year) and (b) allowing U.S. companies to use IFRS. The Concept Release noted,

> The use of a single set of accounting standards in the preparation of financial statements could help investors understand investment opportunities better than the use of multiple differing sets of national accounting standards. Without a single set of accounting standards, global investors must incur time, costs and effort to understand companies' financial statements so that they can adequately compare investment opportunities.[3]

The SEC added that using common standards can also lower costs for issuers. Before such standardization, they must prepare financial statements using different sets of accounting standards. Such costs include the costs of learning the requirements in multiple jurisdictions and keeping current with them.

Ray Ball, of the University of Chicago, has observed that there are other factors pushing countries toward IFRS:

> Accounting is shaped by economics and politics, so the source of international convergence in accounting standards is increased cross-border integration of markets and politics. Driving this integration is an extraordinary reduction in the cost of international communication and transacting. The cumulative effect of innovations affecting almost all dimensions of information costs . . . is a revolutionary plunge in the cost of being informed about and becoming an actor in the markets and politics of other countries. . . . We have witnessed a revolutionary internationalisation of both markets and politics, and inevitably this creates a demand for international convergence in reporting.[4]

David Damant, an internationally well-known Certified Financial Analyst, commenting on Professor Ball's remarks, has added that another benefit is that "many billions will be saved by the fact that scarce capital is no longer invested in the wrong places at the wrong times." His argument is that increased comparability will enhance investor decision making, leading to greater efficiency. He adds, "It is hard to imagine any other technical device, in the hands of very few specialist professionals, which could have such a widespread beneficial effect on the world as a whole."[5]

Professor Ball cites a number of other advantages. He notes that having a worldwide standard would help small investors to compete better with professionals and reduces the risk of adverse selection of investments. It reduces the cost of processing financial information and, in particular, of putting it into large, standardized-format databases. He thinks that reducing the cost of information processing could increase market efficiency (i.e., in the context of the Efficient Market Hypothesis concerning the extent to which information is impounded in share prices). It would also remove some barriers to cross-border acquisitions and disposals. He sums up, "In general, IFRS offer increased comparability and hence reduced information costs and information risk to investors."[6] This should in turn lead to reduced costs of equity capital.

However, Professor Ball suggests that IFRS enforcement will be uneven around the world: "Substantial international differences in financial reporting practice and financial reporting are inevitable, international standards or no international standards. This conclusion is based on the premise that—despite increased globalization—most political and economic influences on reporting *practice* remain local." He is concerned that investors will be misled into believing that there is more uniformity in practice than actually is the case.

The SEC's Concept Release notes that securities' market regulators work within national boundaries but says,

> Because it is likely that not everyone will apply accounting standards consistently or appropriately, securities regulators are developing infrastructure to identify and address the application of IFRS globally. This infrastructure, which starts with IOSCO, is designed to foster the consistent and faithful application of IFRS around the world.

David Damant considers that investors will exert continual pressure, implicitly and explicitly, in favor of the correct implementation of IFRS. He says that investors will demand a higher return on their funds if this is not done.

Overall, the argument for worldwide adoption of a single set of financial reporting standards is that it increases efficiency: it makes it easier for investors to make decisions, it makes those decisions better because company performance can be compared outside of national boundaries, and it supports a global capital market. For accountants and auditors, it creates a knowledge base that can be used in many different countries without retraining. For multinational companies, it will mean that subsidiaries can report locally with the same GAAP as the parent reports globally.

Barry Melancon, president of the AICPA, told *The CPA Letter*, "The AICPA supports one set of high-quality global accounting standards for public companies. We believe the capital markets ultimately will insist on IFRS for public companies."[7]

Bob Herz, chairman of the FASB has said,

> We are creating what we think is both better GAAP and common GAAP across the major capital markets. That's the objective, that's the vision, and we think that's very important to world economic growth and will also benefit U.S. investors. That's a big positive.[8]

## The IASB/FASB Convergence Program

The United States has been involved with the international standard-setter since it was formed. Wally Olson, president of the AICPA from 1972 to 1980 participated in the original meeting between representatives of professional accounting bodies from Canada, the United Kingdom, and the United States in 1972 at which the project was first discussed (for details, see chapter 6) and the AICPA supplied the first secretary (Paul Rosenfield, who had previously been working with AICPA's Accounting Principles Board) when the International Accounting Standards Committee (IASC) opened its doors in 1973.

In the Anglo-Saxon accounting world, it was normal for the professional bodies to provide the national standard-setter, and the IASC followed that model when it was set up. The creation of the FASB, also in 1973, was the first step away from this model and toward the use of professional standard-setters. Over time this became a trend, and in 1988 the IASC invited the FASB to participate in its work.[9] FASB members cannot sit as voting members on the boards of other bodies, so their participation was formally that of a guest member. The Financial Accounting Foundation, the FASB's oversight body, revised the FASB's mission statement in 1991 to include the promotion of internationally comparable accounting standards.

In 1991, the FASB published its "Plan for International Activities," which provided for an extension of its activities with the IASC, citing the "explosive growth of cross-border financing and investing." However, Camfferman and Zeff suggest, "Another impelling factor may have been the swift rise of the SEC's interest in international harmonization and specifically in the role being played by the IASC."[10]

In 1994 the FASB, IASC, and Canada worked together to produce new standards on earnings per share, as they also later attempted to do on segment reporting. In 1995 the FASB revised its Plan for International Activities, noting that it had become apparent that "international issues are so intertwined with domestic issues that there is no way to clearly separate the two."[11]

The IASC Board ceased activities in 2000 to be replaced by the IASB, which started work in April 2001. In October, the IASB held its first board meeting in Washington, DC, and included sessions with the FASB. In September of the following year, the IASB and FASB met at the latter's headquarters in Norwalk, Connecticut, for the first of what was to become a regular sequence of meetings every 6 months beginning in 2004. In the margins of that meeting, the two boards negotiated what is known as the "Norwalk Agreement," setting out the basis of a joint work program to produce converged standards.

The Norwalk Agreement provided for future joint development of new standards and also worked to eliminate differences in existing standards. As IASB chairman David Tweedie said in evidence to a U.S. Senate subcommittee in October 2007, "Both the SEC and the FASB have been actively engaged in our work from the very beginning, and the FASB and the IASB have established joint work programes."

Among the early products of this work was the Statement of Financial Accounting Standards (SFAS) 123(R), which the FASB issued in the context of the IASB issuing its IFRS 2 *Share Based Payment*. This standard required entities to recognize the fair value of share options in the income statement when the option was granted. The FASB had run into political problems when it first issued SFAS 123 and thus had to make key parts of it optional. These became compulsory when the standard was revised. The IASB, for its part, issued IFRS 5 *Non-current Assets Held for Sale and Discontinued Operations*. This aligned international standards with SFAS 144 *Accounting for the Impairment or Disposal of Long-Lived Assets*. The two boards also set out on a long-term project to update their conceptual frameworks and in doing so to create a common framework.

The 2006 Memorandum of Understanding signaled the next phase of convergence between the FASB and the IASB. This was a continuation of the Norwalk Agreement program, but this time the memorandum was written in the context of the roadmap agreed between the chairman of the SEC and the European commissioner responsible for the internal market. The roadmap set out a plan whereby the FASB and IASB would continue to work on convergence, and, subject to satisfactory progress, the SEC would remove the 20-F reconciliation requirement for foreign issuers using IFRS.

The 20-F reconciliation (where foreign SEC registrants have to reconcile earnings and equity under home GAAP to what the figures would have been under U.S. GAAP) is seen as a major cost for foreign companies wanting a secondary listing in the United States. Its removal had long been a target of the IASC and was subsequently pursued vigorously by the IASB.

The 2006 Memorandum of Understanding set out a detailed series of milestones that the SEC thought the two standard-setters should be able to meet by the end of 2007. However, the emphasis was more on the SEC wanting to be reassured that there was an effective process in place through which convergence was continuing and not so much on the achievement of converged standards in key areas.

In any event, the SEC went ahead in June 2007 with a proposal to eliminate the 20-F reconciliation for companies using IFRS as issued by the IASB. The August 2007 Concept Release noted,

> Convergence is the approach that for the last five years has been at work to align the financial reporting of U.S. issuers under U.S. GAAP with that of companies using IFRS. If there is a robust and active process in place for converging IFRS and U.S. GAAP, then it is likely that the current differences between them will be minimized in due course.

The standard-setters continued to work on achieving their milestones under the 2006 Memorandum of Understanding, although the immediate hurdle had been crossed. In 2008 they issued a revised Memorandum of Understanding setting out milestones that they aimed to complete by 2011. This date is significant because Canada, China, Japan, Brazil, India, and Korea have programs in place to adopt IFRS by 2011. The IASB is keen that companies in these countries should not face an immediate change to standards they had just adopted. Its strategy is therefore to complete major joint projects in time for these companies to adopt the new standards immediately. They will then be given a standstill period (as was the case in 2005) during which no new standards will have mandatory effective dates. This could be for up to 3 years, which would make 2014 the next key date, at which point the United States might start to move to IFRS.

## The Fruits of Convergence

The first obvious signs of convergence were the standards on expensing share options and on disclosure of discontinued operations. However, when the IASB first started work, it set out on a rapid improvement program for the existing international accounting standards, taking the opportunity to converge where this was easily possible. It also undertook a revision of its business combinations standard. This resulted in the issue of IFRS 3 in 2004. The new standard, as well as amendments to others, aligned IFRS with the approach in SFAS 141 *Business Combinations* and SFAS 142 *Goodwill and Other Intangible Assets*. The two boards then set out together on phase II of the revision of business combinations leading to the 2007 amendments to SFAS 141 and IFRS 3.

Subsequently, the IASB issued IFRS 8, a straight importation of SFAS 131 *Disclosures About Segments of an Enterprise and Related Information* into an IFRS context. It also amended the relevant standard to require companies to provide details of Other Comprehensive Income in the context of the renamed Income Statement (now the Statement of Comprehensive Income). The IASB had, in revising IAS 39 on recognition and measurement of financial instruments, introduced a fair value option. This allowed companies to opt to use fair value through the income statement for financial instruments to correct and account for mismatch between assets and liabilities, or because they managed their exposures that way. This was reflected and expanded in SFAS 159 *The Fair Value Option for Financial Assets and Financial Liabilities*.

Under the Memorandum of Understanding as revised for the 2011 target, there are a number of significant projects that are supposed to be finished. These include a new standard on liabilities and equity, where the FASB has been taking a lead. The IASB must also issue its version of SFAS 157 *Fair Value Measurement*. Both standard-setters are working on new consolidation standards, but the IASB standard also covers variable interest entities (in U.S. GAAP these are covered separately in FASB Interpretation 46 Revised). They have a joint project on financial statement presentation and the IASB is leading a joint project on leasing. The two boards aim to complete a long-running project on revenue recognition by 2011. They are also working on derecognition of financial instruments.

The IASB has a plan to update its postretirement benefits (IAS 19). The aim is to remove the option to smooth actuarial gains and losses by 2011. This would bring it broadly into line with U.S. GAAP, while the two boards work on a major review of pensions. The long-term project should result in a common standard by 2014. The IASB is also planning to amend its standard for income taxes. The amendments will address a number of convergence problems, but the specifics of the U.S. legal framework and the absence of country-specific issues in the international standard mean that full convergence will not be achieved. The respective approaches of the U.S. and the IASB start from the same principle but differ at the level of detail.

## The Role of the SEC

The SEC has played a major role in shaping the world of converging accounting standards. It has been active in different contexts. In particular the SEC has been a key player in the work of IOSCO. It originated in 1974 as an inter-American regional association of national securities market regulators. Its members decided in 1983 to become a global body and welcomed its first non-American members in 1984.

An important early initiative was to establish a unique listing requirement worldwide for the secondary listings of multinational companies. In many countries, foreign issuers had to meet domestic listing requirements that applied to primary listings. This meant that secondary listings could involve preparation of multiple sets of financial statements and different disclosures in different markets. The IOSCO's idea was that the regulator in the market of primary listing should be the lead regulator, and there should be a single reporting and disclosure package that was acceptable worldwide for secondary listings.

This idea was set out in a 1989 report from the No. 1 Working Party of IOSCO's Technical Committee and endorsed at the 1990 annual meeting. But while the working party was looking at the subject, the SEC had informally suggested to the IASC that they should get involved with this initiative. Clearly there was a role in supplying the accounting standards that would be the backbone of the international reporting package.

It was also in the late 1980s that the SEC was making key policy announcements nationally, as discussed earlier in this chapter, and establishing a commitment to high-quality international standards.

The SEC continued to be active both directly by responding to IASC papers and indirectly through IOSCO. The SEC set out its position on IOSCO and international accounting standards in a report mandated by Congress that was published in October 1997.[12] It noted that the SEC "is committed to providing the necessary input to achieve the goal of establishing a comprehensive set of international accounting standards." The report noted,

> These activities have required a significant commitment of staff resources. In the Office of the Chief Accountant, three accountants focus primarily on international accounting issues. This office also has just hired a fourth accountant to work primarily on international accounting, reporting and auditing issues. Staff members of the Office of the Chief Accountant spent over 4,000 hours working in this area in the fiscal year ended September 30, 1997.

The 1997 report also noted that there were concerns about the IASC's structure but observed that there was a Strategy Working Party that was working on a different structure for the future. The chairman of the Strategy Working Party was Ed Waitzer, a former chairman of the Ontario Securities Commission. Other members included Tony Cope, a member of the U.S. Financial Accounting Standards Board, and David Ruder, a former chairman of the SEC. David Tweedie, then chairman of the UK standard-setter, was also a member.

The future structure of the standard-setter was a highly controversial subject, with a polarization between those who wanted an inclusive, geographically representative body and those who wanted a small, professional committee. Camfferman and Zeff report that the SEC chief accountant at the time, Lynn Turner, "was uncompromising in his support of the small, full-time, independent expert model exemplified in the FASB's structure and process." He told the IASC chairman and secretary general "that the SEC would reject the constituency model categorically."[13]

In the end the new structure included a standard-setter (the IASB) with 14 members. The SEC did not get quite as small a board as it would have liked but was decisive in ensuring that the IASB was modeled on the FASB and was not a large representative body as the IASC had been.

More publicly, following the completion of the core standards agreed between IOSCO and the IASC, the SEC in 2000 issued a Concept Release setting out a series of questions about the possible acceptance of international accounting standards. In 2002 the SEC officially welcomed the Norwalk Agreement on convergence of standards between the FASB and the IASB. In 2003, the SEC published a study, ordered by the Sarbanes-Oxley Act, on principles-based accounting standards. The study suggested that objectives-based standards with application guidance were more desirable than standards with bright lines such as those the FASB put out. In 2006, SEC chairman Christopher Cox publicly agreed with EU commissioner Charlie McCreevy on a roadmap that would lead to removal of the 20-F Reconciliation for foreign registrants using IFRS as issued by the IASB.

During these last years the SEC was also gaining more and more experience working with the financial statements of companies reporting under IFRS. As noted in the 2007 Concept Release, the SEC had 110 filings under IFRS in 2006 and about 70 filings using a "jurisdictional variation" of IFRS. Through IOSCO, the SEC participates in a device to keep regulators informed of each other's rulings in respect of IFRS. IOSCO has set up a database in which securities regulators can file details of rulings they have made in relation to individual sets of financial statements prepared under IFRS.

As discussed earlier, one potential problem of non-jurisdiction-specific global standards is that application guidance might vary from one country to another. The international audit networks address this through global

IFRS offices that coordinate efforts between national offices. Securities regulators are addressing this through the publication of their decisions.

The SEC continues to work with the IASB, on both a formal and an informal level. It is an observer on both the SAC and the IFRIC. It has a deputy chief accountant, Julie Erhardt, dedicated to international standards, and it comments on IASB discussion papers and exposure drafts. Since 2009, it has had a place on a new Monitoring Board that oversees the overall governance of the international standards structure.

IFRS are far from unknown territory for the SEC. The U.S. initiative to create IOSCO in the 1980s has been followed by a commitment by the securities regulator to the development of a global set of high-quality financial reporting standards. The SEC worked both through IOSCO and directly with the IASC in the 1990s to develop and refine the IASC's product. The SEC has also worked behind the scenes to influence the IASC's strategic thinking. In this century it has strongly supported convergence between IASB and FASB standards and is committed to the goal of a single set of GAAP for the world's capital markets.

When SEC chief accountant Conrad Hewitt stood down in January 2009, he left on record that, in his view, the initiative to move to IFRS was "the most important accounting policy decision ever made by the Commission." He added,

> In all of the Commission's work to date, a consistent premise has been that investors are better served by having available high quality financial information across issuers, regardless of their domicile. This aids investors in making informed decisions in allocating their capital among competing alternatives.[14]

## The FASB's Position

As we have seen, the FASB moved to an international involvement about 20 years ago and started participating in the work of the IASC at that time. The FASB staff worked on IASC projects during the 1990s. An FASB member was a member of the IASC's Strategy Working Party. When the new IASB was formed, the FASB was again much involved. Of the 14 members of the IASB at the inaugural meeting in April 2001, 2 (Tony Cope and Jim Leisenring) were former FASB members.

Three others—Mary Barth, Tom Jones, and Bob Herz—had previously been involved with the U.S. standard-setting process in different ways. Tricia O'Malley, a former chairman of the Canadian Accounting Standards Committee, was also one the original members of the international board. The IASB's first director of research was Wayne Upton, previously a senior staff member at the FASB. The relationship between the two standard-setting boards was further cemented in 2002 when IASB member Bob Herz was appointed chairman of the FASB.

Mr. Herz appeared before the Subcommittee on Securities, Insurance, and Investment of the Senate Committee on Banking, Housing and Urban Affairs on October 24, 2007. He told the subcommittee, "The ultimate goal, we believe, is a common, high-quality, global financial reporting system that can be used for decision-making purposes across the capital markets of the world." He added,

> We believe reaching this ideal financial reporting system would significantly improve the overall usefulness and comparability of reported financial information, increase investor confidence, and reduce the complexity and costs investors and companies face, resulting in global capital markets that function more efficiently.

Mr. Herz warned, however, that this ideal situation was still some time away. He said that there must be improvements to and convergence of the infrastructure supporting the international capital markets. There needed to be high-quality accounting standards, a well-funded global standard-setter, and a global interpretative body. But there also had to be improvements to disclosure requirements, to enforcement and regulatory regimes, to auditing standards, and to the education of market participants.

He pointed out that the challenges included differences in institutional, regulatory, business, and cultural environments. There was resistance to change, differing priorities among jurisdictions, and existing U.S. demand for detailed guidance and specialized industry standards. He noted, though, "We believe the benefits the ideal system offers, however, well justify the cost and effort of confronting these many challenges."

In terms of convergence, he suggested that while significant progress had been made, the work was incomplete and it would be appropriate to consider how to accelerate the convergence effort. He said, "Planning for a transition of U.S. public companies to an improved version of IFRS would be an effective and logical way forward to achieving the goal of a set of common global standards."

Overall, the FASB's position could be summed up as a commitment to a single set of global standards, as well as a commitment to convergence with IFRS to achieve those standards. However, there should be an orderly process over several years during which changes are brought about in the infrastructure and improvements made to IFRS. Thereafter, U.S. listed companies should move to IFRS.

It is too early to say what the role of the FASB would be after 2014 should the SEC decide to require registrants to use IFRS. Mr. Herz's testimony did not address that question, but national standard-setters in Europe have continued to function since 2005. In many jurisdictions they also have a role in specifying standards for private companies. The larger national standard-setters, such as those of Germany, Britain, France, and Australia, have retained their technical staff and work with IASB staff on developing future projects. They also liaise with the IFRIC.

## The SEC's Proposed Rule

On November 14, 2008, the SEC published its proposed rule for moving to IFRS (Release No.33-8982) and asked for comments on it.[15] The roadmap sets out seven milestones toward the adoption of IFRS instead of U.S. GAAP. It proposes that certain companies could move voluntarily in 2009; a decision would be reached in 2011, and if this was positive, the largest registrants would move in 2014, followed by two further waves in 2015 and 2016. It should be noted, though, that incoming SEC chairman Mary Schapiro said in her confirmation hearings in January 2009 that she supported a single global standard, but she was not willing to be bound by the timetable in the proposed rule.

The main idea of the proposed rule is that there should be a staggered adoption process. This would be based on the existing SEC classifications of "large accelerated filers," "accelerated filers," and then the remaining registrants. Assuming a positive decision is reached in 2011, large accelerated filers would move in 2014, accelerated filers in 2015, and everyone else in 2016. The proposal does not include any relaxation of the requirement to provide 3 years' financial statements, so large accelerated filers would have to start capturing data suitable for IFRS from January 2012, very shortly after the decision on the proposed timetable.

The proposed rule says,

> Our current expectation that an issuer's status as an accelerated filer could determine the date of a required transition to IFRS is based on the premise that larger issuer would be better able to allocate resources to the transition to IFRS more quickly than smaller issuers, and a staged transition also may help manage the resource demands on auditors, consultants and other market participants.[16]

The proposal notes that a disadvantage of this approach is that it "would embed non-comparability among the issuers within an industry." It says that the commission will consider at a later stage whether, in such a situation, a filer can elect an earlier transition date to remain comparable.

A significant part of the suggested transition allows certain multinational companies that meet specific criteria to elect to adopt IFRS voluntarily in 2009. Here the commission suggests that if a U.S. issuer is among the 20 largest companies globally in a particular industry, and IFRS is used as the basis of financial reporting more often than any other basis among the top 20 largest listed companies worldwide, the issuer would be eligible to use IFRS.[17] The company would have to apply to the SEC for a staff letter stating that the SEC had no objection to filing under IFRS.

The SEC staff estimates that in 34 of approximately 74 industry sectors considered, the condition of IFRS being the dominant reporting basis would likely be met. It also estimated that approximately 110 U.S. multinationals would be in a position to apply for voluntary adoption.

However, the costs for the early adopters could be significant. They would still be obliged to provide 3 years of audited financial statements, which would mean preparing IFRS statements for 2007 and 2008 retrospectively. They would also have to provide some form of reconciliation with U.S. GAAP, although two options are put forward. The SEC says,

We believe that U.S. GAAP financial information, whether presented under either proposal, would be useful to investors in order to facilitate their understanding of and education with respect to IFRS during the early stages of transition of U.S. issuers to IFRS. This reconciliation, under either Proposal, would assist investors in their understanding and appreciation of the differences between U.S. GAAP and IFRS as issued by the IASB as such differences relate to the issuer providing disclosure.[18]

The SEC has estimated the costs of a company adopting IFRS early as approximately $32 million for the first 3 years where there is a 10-K filing. It has based its estimates on the 110 companies it had tentatively identified for early adoption. It looked at the ICAEW study of adoption in Europe (see chapter 1) and concluded that U.S. costs would be higher because of different U.S. filing requirements, "which require, among other things, issuers to include 3 years of audited financial statements, and our requirements related to internal controls over financial reporting." The SEC assumes that the bulk of the cost would fall in the first year.

Aside from setting out the proposed transitional arrangements, should the United States decide to move to IFRS, the proposed rule also includes a number of milestones related to progress with IFRS and convergence. It says that it will continue to monitor the joint work program of the FASB and IASB and would want assurance that they will make progress on converging standards. It also wants assurance that the IASB would be an efficient and effective standard-setter, while accepting that U.S. influence would be less than its influence on the FASB because of the other countries involved.

Regarding the governance of the IASB, the proposed rule calls for enhanced SEC oversight, as the trustees had already proposed. This was formally put in place at the beginning of 2009 with the creation of a Monitoring Board on which the chairman of the SEC has a seat. Its proposal also says that the SEC must be satisfied that the IASB has secure and stable funding for the foreseeable future. The FASB was given mandatory funding under the 2002 Sarbanes-Oxley Act, but for nearly 30 years before that it depended on voluntary contributions, a model that the IASB currently uses.

The SEC would also want to see improved Extensible Business Reporting Language (XBRL) tagging for IFRS data. It called for the existing IFRS tagging to be extended into a much more detailed version comparable to what U.S. issuers would be using. The commission would also monitor progress on education. It notes,

> The need for IFRS training would involve personnel of issuers, their governing bodies, such as audit committees, and their auditors. Such requirements for training also extend to specialists, such as actuaries and valuation experts, since these professionals are engaged by management to assist in measuring certain assets and liabilities, and likely are not currently proficient in IFRS. Professional associations and industry groups would need to integrate IFRS into their training materials, publications, testing and certification programs. Colleges and universities would need to include IFRS in their curricula.[19]

The proposed rule specifies that the SEC would take into account the then status of the overall education, training, and readiness of investors, preparers, auditors, and other parties involved.

The proposed rule was issued in 2008 during the last months of the Bush administration. Since then President Obama has moved into the White House, and there has been a change at the top of the SEC. SEC chairman Christopher Cox has stepped down to be replaced by Mary Schapiro, who already served 6 years as an SEC commissioner from 1988 to 1994.

At her confirmation hearing in front of the Senate Banking Committee in January 2009, she said she would proceed with great caution on IFRS. She thought that a single set of global standards would be "a very beneficial thing" but expressed concerns about the lack of detail in IFRS. She also expressed concerns at the IASB's independence. She said she was not sure that the $30 million cost estimate was a necessary expense in the current economic climate. She said, "I will take a big, deep breath and look at this entire area again carefully," adding, "I will not necessarily feel bound by the existing roadmap that is out for comment."[20]

The rule proposed in November had a comment deadline of January 30, 2009. A number of corporations, such as Boeing and Eli Lilly, wrote to the SEC pointing out that they were in the middle of their year-end reporting exercise at that time and asking for an extension of the deadline. This was given in February, pushing the deadline to April 20.

However, a number of U.S. corporations have now responded as of March 2009, including FedEx, Dell, IBM, ExxonMobil, and Hertz. John Merino, chief accounting officer of FedEx, says the company supports a single set of standards but "we do not believe IFRS has yet demonstrated that it can achieve the status of a single set of high quality globally accepted accounting standards."[21] Mr. Merino suggests that convergence should be substantially complete before going ahead. He also pointed out that requiring 3 years of comparative data is impractical and would require considerable expense. He suggests FedEx's conversion costs could be nearer $50 million without taking in education and training.

Thomas Sweet, chief accounting officer of Dell, comments that "the evolving global economy has created the need for an international language of disclosure and transparency to protect investors and promote comparability of corporate financials." However, he suggests that a 2011 decision requiring companies to collect data in 2012 is not practical. He thinks a 5-year process is more realistic. Nor does he think it is realistic to suggest some companies could adopt early, given that there is no certainty that the United States would go to IFRS: "There needs to be certainty in the implementation date."[22]

He also underlines the need for a stable platform of IFRS before conversion. He says the FASB and IASB have 11 major projects before them, and they need to focus on "the critical few we believe will derive the optimal benefit."

IBM's Greg Nelson supports the proposal. He says, "These standards will enable investors to compare companies across national boundaries, enhance the efficiency of capital markets worldwide, improve the quality of information reported in various jurisdictions and reduce the burden and cost of compliance with multiple reporting frameworks."[23]

At a detailed level, Mr. Nelson thinks the commission's milestones for progress by the IASB and FASB may negatively impact the process, leading to confusion, because of the magnitude of the changes proposed. The company is, though, concerned that postponing a decision until 2011 may cause companies to delay necessary preparation beyond an acceptable time-frame: "We strongly encourage the Commission to decide as soon as pos-sible on a final Roadmap and not defer its decision until 2011."

Patrick Mulva at ExxonMobil notes that the company would be eli-gible to file IFRS statements as an early adopter. However, the company sees "significant disincentives" to do so. In the absence of a date certain for a mandatory adoption, they would be unwilling to make the major investment necessary: "The cost of this effort for ExxonMobil is expected to be significant, running into tens of millions of dollars." They say the costs outweigh the potential benefits, and the company is worried about the adverse tax effects of not being able to use Last In First Out (LIFO).[24]

The Hertz Corporation believes adoption should wait until "the two sets of standards are sufficiently converged [so that] there will be no need to choose one set of standards over the other." However, they also think that companies should not be restricted in choosing to go to IFRS early if they wish to do so.[25]

## Advantages and Disadvantages for U.S. Companies

Of course, it will be costly for U.S. companies to switch to a different basis of accounting, even if it is very close to U.S. GAAP. Staff will have to be retrained, software will have to be changed, and there will likely be a period of uncertainty as the new system beds down. There is a one-off transitional cost that will spread over 2 to 5 years. Will the benefits there-after justify that?

The pros and cons of moving to IFRS affect different companies dif-ferently. A company with a significant international activity that is listed on several stock exchanges has the most to gain. In a world that is moving rapidly toward IFRS as the global standard, even if GAAP is accepted as the basis of accounting outside the United States, a U.S. company will start to find that investors will prefer to see the result measured compara-bly with competitors. Investors will be up to date in their knowledge of IFRS but less so in their knowledge of U.S. GAAP and may discount the price because of that extra element of uncertainty.

If U.S. GAAP were not accepted as the basis of accounting on a foreign exchange, then U.S. issuers listed on foreign exchanges would have to prepare additional information or even full financials on a different basis—perhaps IFRS. All multinationals operate through national subsidiaries, and these are required to file individual company accounts locally. A company with many foreign subsidiaries will find that in many countries they can file their local accounts according to IFRS. If these could drop straight into the consolidation of group accounts, that would remove an extra complication—and a lot of extra cost—from preparing worldwide financial statements.

A single accounting standard throughout the world would bring a number of other benefits for multinationals. For example, at the moment their accounting cadres and internal audit teams must be able to look at accounts prepared on different bases as they move from post to post in the worldwide group. In an IFRS world, training costs would be dramatically reduced, staff could transfer more easily around the group, and there would be a better understanding by accountants and managers of the group's figures. Some companies achieve this position by using U.S. GAAP around the world, but they are still obliged to rework the data in each country where they have a subsidiary. That second layer of cost would disappear.

However, if you are an SEC registrant whose activities are limited to the United States and you have no foreign investors, the costs may look more significant than the benefits. Initially you would have to retrain staff, ensure that your auditor was up to speed on IFRS (and if that's not the case, you might have to switch auditors), and help your core investors to understand what was happening to your financial statements.

Even so, the European experience shows that many companies with no obvious immediate benefit have been quite keen to follow IFRS. One argument advanced is that a company retaining local GAAP looks as though it has no aspirations and is not interested in expanding or being part of the global market. While you may not be seeking foreign investors, once your figures are in IFRS, you may well find that investors come looking for you. If you take the IFRS effect alongside the move to tagging financial data under XBRL, investors worldwide will be able to call up your numbers and compare them. The IASB was an early participant in the XBRL movement and has a permanent team providing annual updates that keep IFRS tags current.

## Challenges to Be Overcome: The Numbers

Individual companies will have to address quite a lot of challenges if the United States moves to IFRS, as will their auditors and the financial analyst community. The first issue is whether a company's financials will look different and what impact that will have on share price. The short answer to that is that (a) yes, in most cases transition will make a difference, and (b) there will be a period of uncertainty once IFRS figures start to be published. Nevertheless, analysts and investors should adjust quite quickly.

The evidence from Europe is that the change impacts different companies differently, and there is some opportunity to mitigate the impact through accounting choices that are taken in making the transition. Many transitional adjustments are taken as a single adjustment to equity. In principle, IFRS 1 *First-Time Adoption of IFRS*, which sets out the way toward transition, requires retrospective application of the standards that are in force at the transition date. That is, companies should adjust their figures as though they had always applied current IFRS.

However, in many instances this is clearly impossible because the data do not exist anymore: you cannot restate in 2013 a business combination that was treated as a merger in 1950 to acquisition accounting. On top of that, IFRS does not accept retrospective determination of fair value. Consequently, the standard contains many compromise solutions to address such issues. Companies have a one-time opportunity to rethink some of their accounting decisions and pass the consequences into equity.

Assuming that the United States followed the proposed rule and moved larger accelerated filers in 2014, a large U.S. company would have to produce the following:

1. 2012 financials under U.S. GAAP in the normal way
2. 2012 financials under IFRS that would be published with the 2014 year-end figures
3. 2013 financials under U.S. GAAP
4. 2013 financials under IFRS, to be published with the 2014 full year

5. A reconciliation of the difference between the 2012 and 2013 figures under U.S. GAAP and the 2012 and 2013 figures under IFRS, also published with the full 2014 figures
6. Full statements, eventually, for 2014 under IFRS with the 2012 and 2013 IFRS comparatives

Companies have to have their IFRS strategy in place well before 2014. Assuming only 2 years of comparatives, a company must assess in 2011 or before what the accounting impact would be and start to prepare its own staff and investors for the move. The company must then prepare its first IFRS balance sheet as of January 1, 2012, and must collect IFRS data thereafter.

IFRS 1 provides a number of voluntary exemptions. These include a choice about how business combinations are treated. IFRS, like U.S. GAAP, only permit use of the acquisition method now, but companies are not obliged to restate all past combinations. They can choose to restate all combinations back to a specified date or not restate any at all. However, in-process research and development, if recognized in a past combination and then written off, might need to be recognized as an intangible asset under IFRS.

Property, plant, and equipment have to be valued as under IFRS, but, where information is not available, fair value or a recent valuation can be used as deemed cost. Investment properties could be held at either fair value or historical cost. Inventory cannot be held on a LIFO basis under IFRS, so LIFO inventory would have to be restated to FIFO or weighted average.

In 2008, the Canadian Accounting Standards Board (AcSB) asked the IASB to revise IFRS 1 to take into account special circumstances occurring in Canada—notably the problem of valuing a large number of small oil deposits individually at fair value. The IASB was willing to help them, and it could reasonably be assumed that any major difficulty identified in the United States in the run up to adoption could also lead to modification of the transitional requirements.

The natural question for preparers is, "Will my bottom line look small in IFRS?" This is impossible to predict because of the combination of different circumstances and different asset-liability mixes. The United Kingdom is arguably the country with accounting nearest to U.S. GAAP in Europe. Aisbitt's analysis of the impact on UK companies of transition,[26] drawn from the 2004 reconciliations between UK GAAP and IFRS statements, gives the figures shown in Table 2.1. Aisbitt linked adjustments back to individual IFRS, as is shown in Table 2.2, where the effects are split between financial institutions and nonfinancial businesses.

It can be seen that the transition involved a lot of small changes for UK companies, rather than any single overriding issue. Retirement obligations were the most significant issue. Many UK companies had been using the "corridor" method to defer recognition of actuarial gains and losses. However, under the transitional arrangements, they were able to

*Table 2.1. Balance Sheet Line Items With Largest Adjustments Following Transfer to IFRS Relative to UK GAAP Equity (Top 20 Items)—Nonfinancial Companies*

| Balance sheet line item | Average change in value of line item expressed as a percentage of UK GAAP equity |
|---|---|
| Retirement benefit obligations [noncurrent] | -15.45 |
| Property plant and equipment | 10.58 |
| Cash and cash equivalents [current] | 8.03 |
| Other financial assets [current] | -7.11 |
| Deferred tax assets [noncurrent] | 6.26 |
| Borrowings [noncurrent] | -5.97 |
| Deferred tax liabilities [noncurrent] | -5.89 |
| Goodwill and intangible assets [noncurrent] | -4.41 |
| Trade and other payables [current] | 3.97 |
| Derivative financial instruments [noncurrent] | 3.80 |
| Trade and other receivables [current] | -3.44 |
| Trade and other receivables [noncurrent] | -3.24 |
| Retirement benefits asset [noncurrent] | 2.88 |
| Provisions for liabilities and charges [noncurrent] | 2.49 |
| Noncurrent assets held for resale | 2.46 |
| Financial instruments—derivatives [current] | -2.29 |
| Trade and other payables [noncurrent] | 2.09 |
| Provisions [current] | -1.89 |
| Current tax liabilities | -1.57 |
| Deferred tax assets [current] | -0.94 |

*Table 2.2. IFRS Adjustments Relative to UK GAAP Equity*

| Accounting standard(s) | Average adjustment expressed as a percentage of UK GAAP equity | | |
|---|---|---|---|
| | MEAN NONFINANCIALS | MEAN FINANCIALS | MEAN ALL |
| IAS 19 and IFRS 2 Employee benefits and Share-based payments (mainly pensions) | -11.74 | -4.22 | -10.10 |
| IAS 10 Events After the Balance Sheet Date | 7.06 | 4.20 | 6.43 |
| IAS 18 Revenue | -5.46 | 0.06 | -4.26 |
| IAS 12 Income tax | -3.93 | -1.58 | -3.42 |
| IAS 16 Property, Plant and Equipment | 4.10 | -0.14 | 3.18 |
| IAS 32/39 Financial Instruments | 2.63 | 0.38 | 2.14 |
| IAS 21 The Effects of Changes in Foreign Exchange Rates | -2.10 | 0.00 | -1.65 |
| IAS 17 Leases | -0.45 | -0.51 | -0.46 |
| Other | 0.51 | -0.51 | 0.29 |
| IAS 37 Provisions | 0.10 | 0.42 | 0.17 |
| IFRS 1 First-Time Adoption | 0.19 | 0.00 | 0.15 |
| IAS 27/36/38 and IFRS 3— group and goodwill stuff | -0.03 | 0.77 | 0.15 |
| IAS 28/31 Interests in Associates and Joint Ventures | 0.12 | 0.02 | 0.10 |
| IFRS 4 Insurance Contracts | 0.00 | -0.47 | -0.10 |
| IFRS 5 Noncurrent Assets Held for Sale and Discontinued Operations | 0.05 | -0.02 | 0.04 |
| IAS 1 Presentation of Financial Statements | 0.00 | -0.01 | 0.00 |
| IAS 11 Construction Contracts | 0.00 | 0.00 | 0.00 |
| IAS 40 Investment Property | 0.00 | -0.02 | 0.00 |
| IAS 41 Biological Assets | 0.00 | 0.00 | 0.00 |

use the option of recognizing all gains and losses at transition, and many of them chose to do this. This resulted in a relatively significant adjustment to equity. U.S. companies would not have the same issue because the FASB withdrew the corridor in 2006. In any event, the international standard is scheduled for amendment before 2011.

However, even if the changes are relatively small, they will impact a company in a number of ways. Investors and analysts will potentially have difficulty interpreting the new figures. This underscores the importance of doing an impact assessment well ahead of the actual transition so users are warned of the likely changes and are reassured that the company has things under control. The larger investment advisers will be working on educating their staff, but it is just as well not to rely on investors making the effort!

Changed figures may also affect internal management accounting and other performance measurement numbers if these are based on the financial reporting system. Changed figures will also impact any contracts that were framed on the basis of U.S. GAAP measurements. Profit-sharing deals, royalties, licenses, any contract based on revenues or profits, or any other accounting number has to be examined to see if IFRS will cause the measurement to change. If so, the contract needs to be renegotiated. The same thing applies to any loan covenants with GAAP-based constraints. The general counsel needs to review all contracts that incorporate GAAP measurements.

A major area for review will be income taxes. IFRS do not permit LIFO, so companies using a LIFO measurement could have a one-time transitional cost. Newall and Kalis reviewed this position in an article in *The Tax Adviser* in June 2008. They speculate that the IASB might change its ban on LIFO but say,

> U.S. companies may no longer be permitted to use LIFO for book and tax reporting purposes (under the conformity rule) unless the current U.S. tax law is changed and the LIFO conformity requirement is eliminated. At present time, there does not appear to be any movement by the IRS, Treasury or Congress to address the LIFO conformity question.

They agree that terminating LIFO could have far-reaching effects and suggest that companies might want to start planning now to manage the transition. They note that the adjustment would be recognized over 4 years under present provisions.

As a general rule, they point out, "It will be important for tax return preparers to understand any differences between the old book reporting method and the IFRS reporting method to ensure the proper treatment for tax reporting purposes." They recommend that tax advisers and internal tax specialists be involved in following the transition from an early stage and that it may be necessary to maintain records that preserve the previous way of accounting for some issues.

A company's numbers are likely to be impacted in many small ways but no major ones. It is important that the company does an impact assessment on a standard by standard basis as early as possible. The results of this should be communicated to investors and analysts to prepare them for the change. At the same time, the different measurements may impact contractual arrangements, loan covenants, and tax positions. Relevant management and advisers should be involved in the transition team at an early stage.

Aaron Anderson, director of IFRS implementation at IBM, has advice for U.S. companies:

> While the accounting differences between IFRS and U.S. GAAP may be significant for your company, there are several fundamental questions that should be answered before this comparison is started.
>
> First, where are you doing IFRS today? If you have operations in Europe, Australia, Israel, China and dozens of other countries around the world, you're likely preparing statutory reports in some form of IFRS already . . . Second, what adjustments are you currently making between your U.S. GAAP books and your statutory books prepared in accordance with IFRS? In most cases, these financial statements are audited and will provide you with a good starting point for determining the GAAP differences impacting your company.[27]

Mr. Anderson also suggests that companies should ask themselves whether they could use the opportunity to introduce other changes, such as increasing standardization, centralization of processes, and economies of scale. He comments that a strong internal cross-functional team "is a key element of a successful IFRS conversion."

## Challenges to Be Overcome: The Costs

Evidently a transition team is essential. This team, in turn, is likely to be one of the major costs. One of the issues that they will have to address is training staff. In Europe a wide range of training schemes were put on the market. Professional bodies such as the Association of Chartered Certified Accountants (ACCA, http://www.accaglobal.com) offer distance learning courses and certificates. Deloitte offers free training modules that can be downloaded from its dedicated IFRS Web site (http://www.iasplus.com). The Big Four audit firms did not get very involved in training, although they were involved in advising companies on their strategy in relation to IFRS adoption.

The SEC's 2007 Concept Release notes,

> All parties would likely need to undertake comprehensive training on IFRS. Professional associations and industry groups would need to integrate IFRS into their training materials, publications, testing and certification programs. Colleges and universities would need to include IFRS in their curricula. Furthermore, eventually it may be appropriate to include IFRS in the Uniform CPA exam.[28]

The ICAEW prepared a report for the European Commission on the costs of the 2005 adoption of IFRS. They compiled data using estimates provided by preparers and auditors who responded to an online survey. In their published report,[29] they divided figures into bands depending on the size of the company based on turnover. For companies with turnover in excess of €5 billion, they said that the average cost of transition was €3.4 million. They provided the analysis of major items shown in Table 2.3.

The report notes that the smallest companies (turnover below €500 million) spent proportionately more on external technical advice and

*Table 2.3. Costs of Transition*

| Item | €'000 |
|---|---|
| IFRS project team | 768 |
| Software and systems changes | 566 |
| External auditing costs | 541 |
| External technical advice | 376 |
| Staff training | 299 |
| Other staff | 271 |
| Communications with third parties | 296 |
| Tax advice | 157 |
| Additional external data costs | 95 |
| Renegotiating debt covenants | 61 |

Source: Adapted from ICAEW (2007), Figure 7.4, p. 67.

external auditing costs. Medium-sized companies also spent more on technical advice, while the largest companies spent more on the project team and software changes.

The ICAEW report gives details of how the respondents' estimates were broken down in relation to areas of accounting (see Table 2.4). It should be noted that the figures quoted in Table 2.4 are estimates from an online survey and are averages of all the responses received. However, they usefully highlight where the main costs are likely to arise. Companies can expect that the IFRS conversion team will be the biggest internal cost, and this will be joined by software and auditing costs as the biggest items with staff training.

## Blueprint for Action

In compiling their report, the ICAEW asked respondents how they could have reduced their implementation costs. The answers provide some insight as to how to better run a transition. They said they could have reduced costs by

- training staff better,
- starting the transition project sooner,
- making a good initial assessment of the impact,
- managing the project more efficiently, and
- communicating better with subsidiaries.

*Table 2.4. Average Implementation Cost by Area of Accounting in €'000*

| Item | Turnover <€500 million | Turnover €500 million–€5,000 million | Turnover >€5,000 million |
|---|---|---|---|
| Derivatives | 56 | 88 | 348 |
| General costs | 48 | 75 | 298 |
| Employee pensions | 44 | 69 | 273 |
| Revenue recognition | 40 | 63 | 249 |
| Financial instruments | 40 | 63 | 249 |
| Consolidation | 36 | 57 | 224 |
| Leases | 32 | 50 | 199 |
| Impairment | 32 | 50 | 199 |
| Goodwill | 28 | 44 | 174 |
| Employee share options | 28 | 44 | 174 |
| Deferred tax | 28 | 44 | 174 |
| Foreign currency | 28 | 44 | 174 |
| Business combinations | 24 | 38 | 149 |
| Debt/Equity | 24 | 38 | 149 |
| Tangible fixed assets | 24 | 38 | 149 |
| Intangible assets | 20 | 31 | 124 |
| Joint ventures | 16 | 25 | 99 |
| Associates | 4 | 6 | 25 |
| Total | 554 | 867 | 3430 |

Source: ICAEW (2007), Table 7.3, p. 69.

It is very difficult for company accountants to take time out from dealing with the problems that concern the current financial year to look 3 or 4 years into the future. However, that is the challenge of transition to IFRS. Leaving aside the special case of the 100 or so companies that the SEC thinks could move early to adopt IFRS, companies should know in 2011 whether they will have to move to IFRS. According to current thinking, the likelihood is that they will have to adopt IFRS. Companies should not wait for 2011 but should (a) make an assessment as to what impact the adoption will have on the financial statements, investors, systems, and contracts, and so on and (b) plan how to carry out the transition as soon as possible based on that impact assessment. When the 2011 decision comes, companies need to have an action plan ready to go.

It would make sense to appoint a senior accountant whose only function is to oversee the predecision stage. There should be an embryo IFRS implementation office that centralizes information about IFRS and accumulates documentation on IFRS. That office will need to subscribe to technical newsletters (e.g., *IFRS Monitor* or *IFRS News*) that report regularly on the evolution of IFRS and ensure that any dedicated material from the auditors is centralized.

The IFRS implementation person, perhaps in liaison with the statutory auditors, should review the areas of difference between IFRS and U.S. GAAP and make an initial assessment of the likely areas where the figures will change and where there will be a need to capture different information. The group may have foreign subsidiaries that are already using IFRS, and their experience with restatement to U.S. GAAP for consolidation purposes may provide insights.

Don Gannon, of Deloitte's IFRS Center of Excellence, suggests,

> While conversion to IFRS on a consolidated basis may be a few years away, companies can start taking advantage now of opportunities to convert to IFRS for statutory reporting purposes overseas. Many countries already permit the use of IFRS. Converting to IFRS for statutory reporting purposes for subsidiaries in those countries may provide an opportunity to develop a multi-year strategy and a detailed roadmap for conversion to IFRS. By leveraging the training and experience gained on these statutory conversions, companies can be better positioned to execute a consolidated IFRS conversion in the future.[30]

The fact that the company is doing an impact assessment should probably be communicated to analysts irrespective of whether the financial statement impact is considered to be significant, but especially if it is thought that it will be material.

After identifying the expected problem areas, there should be an assessment of what systems changes might be needed (including potentially internal controls) and what staff training will be needed. This assessment should be communicated groupwide, and controllers of subsidiaries, as well as managers in areas that might be effected (such as taxation), should be invited to comment and discuss the impact on their area.

There should also be discussions with the auditors about their state of readiness to audit IFRS statements and any special requirements they are likely to have.

In an ideal world the company should start a process of training controllers in IFRS, probably using off-the-shelf packages such as that of the ACCA or using the AICPA's IFRS resources center (http://www.ifrs .com). When 2011 comes, there will be a scramble for training and a need for experienced staff. It would be better to use the predecision period to ensure that selected, key financial accounting staff have done IFRS training at (relatively) quiet periods in the year so that knowledge is already trickling through the system. A full-scale training program should also be designed so that other accounting staff can then be brought up to speed as soon as the go-ahead is given.

You should remember that the European experience was that many companies did not plan ahead early enough and did not start their training until 2003, even though they needed an IFRS statement of financial position by January 1, 2004. They faced stiff competition for scarce resources, and suppliers of training and software were reluctant to increase capacity because they knew demand would melt away in 2005. Certainly, in training staff early there is some risk of waste, either because implementation is delayed or abandoned or because staff are poached by other companies. However, the costs of not being ready are likely to be higher, and special arrangements can be made with key staff to ensure they are retained over the implementation period. Neither group management nor investors are likely to be happy with an accounting staff that is less than comfortable recognizing the impact of transition and managing it smoothly.

Once the green light is given, the company should step up its efforts. An implementation coordination group should be formed that involves every department likely to be effected. The Implementation Office should start preparing internal briefing documents for managers. The wider staff training program should be implemented and detailed specifications should be drawn up for changes to systems, including software and internal controls.

Supposing that 2014 is the possible transition date—and that IFRS figures are needed for 2012—the company should, by the end of 2011, be well on the way to implementing the changes so that they can be tested and corrected if necessary. This is a tough objective and underlines why it is necessary to do a lot of preliminary analysis before 2011—and why some respondents to the proposed rule are saying it is unrealistic or calling for an earlier decision date. Nevertheless, such timely implementation and testing will enable managers to see what impact the changes would likely have on financial information used internally by the company and given to external stakeholders.

One issue that should not be forgotten is that the transition to IFRS is a moving target. Likely changes before 2014 are predictable (see chapter 4) but the Implementation Office needs to monitor the IASB and stay up to date with changes. If it thinks the company will be badly affected by IFRS, then the earlier this can be flagged to the FASB and the IASB, the greater the possibility of smoothing out rough edges.

The key to a successful transition is to start as early as possible and make a detailed impact assessment. That assessment needs to be communicated widely, both within the worldwide group and to external stakeholders. It should also give rise to a sequenced plan to train staff progressively and change systems if necessary. Leaving everything to the last minute is a big temptation, not least because general management usually do not think they should have to spend any money on accounting; but money spent early is much more money saved later and uncertainty avoided.

## Conclusion

The generally accepted wisdom among key decision makers in U.S. financial reporting is that a move to more widely accepted, less rules-based standards is desirable. It will have costs for preparers to make the transition, as well as for auditors and professional investors who will need to do special training. However, the benefits in terms of comparability and improved efficiency of investment are expected to well outweigh the costs. Most likely, companies will benefit directly as well since many foreign subsidiaries will be able to, or be required to, report under IFRS for local filing purposes. Companies may take this opportunity to improve and harmonize their worldwide reporting systems.

The effect of using IFRS should not be that extreme in that they are close to U.S. GAAP in many areas, but the impact on each company is likely to be different because of the different mix of activities, assets, and liabilities of each. However, the costs of transition will be lessened, and the uncertainties will be reduced, if companies start their impact assessment well before 2011. They need to create a well-informed, well-documented IFRS Implementation Unit under a senior accountant, and this person should carry out an impact assessment as soon as possible. The impact assessment will be the blueprint for a successful transition. Once a company has identified the problem areas, it can put plans in place to address them.

Available external resources for training, software, and other advice are likely to be under a lot of pressure in 2012 and 2013. It is advisable to train selected senior accountants before 2011, and then put the full IFRS Implementation Program into gear as soon as the SEC makes its decision. However, that is a difficult decision to make in the absence of certainty. One hopes that the SEC makes an earlier decision.

# CHAPTER 3

# Canadian GAAP and IFRS

Canadian listed companies have always had an ambivalent approach to IFRS for the very good reason that their nearest and biggest trading partner is the United States, and so U.S. GAAP has been a major influence. At a conference in Toronto in October 2003—attended by both Bob Herz from the FASB and David Tweedie from the IASB—David Brown, chairman of the Ontario Securities Commission, said that he did not see Canada going down the European route and endorsing IFRS. Others said Canadian companies could not ignore the U.S. markets.[1]

On the other hand, Canada was one of the founding countries that created the original IASC and has played a big role in the development of the standards—and in particular the financial instruments standard IAS 39. Consequently, Canadian GAAP has links to both U.S. GAAP and IFRS. After an extensive consultation program, the AcSB announced in January 2006 that publicly accountable companies would switch in 2011 to IFRS. As Paul Cherry, chairman of the AcSB, put it, "Many participants in the Canadian capital markets were becoming increasingly uncomfortable with Canadian standards that were neither one thing nor the other—that is, neither IFRS nor U.S. GAAP, but a mix of both."[2]

## The Canadian Transition Plan

The AcSB made its first announcement on the transition in 2006, saying that this was a preliminary decision that would be subject to confirmation in 2008, with the changeover date penciled in for 2011. At the same time they made it understood that there was little likelihood of the plan not going ahead and companies were encouraged to start thinking about transition straight away and not wait until 2008. Clearly, the SEC has been more cautious, saying only that a decision will be made in 2011. In the United States, some companies may adopt early as an experiment but are expected to maintain U.S.GAAP figures in case the SEC decides not to go to IFRS. Evidently, U.S. companies have a less clear message and may hesitate about what resources to commit ahead of 2011.

Part of the Canadian plan was to separate accounting for privately held companies from that of publicly accountable ones. The idea is that privately held companies would have the opportunity to move to IFRS if they wished. It is expected that a number of private companies will do so, in particular those that are part of international groups in which IFRS is used predominantly, those that are parents or subsidiaries, and those considering going public in the near future. The AcSB is developing a separate GAAP for private companies based on existing Canadian GAAP. However, companies that were SEC registrants would still have the option of using U.S. GAAP instead.

Why did Canada want to change? Paul Cherry's answer is,

Because Canada cannot stand in isolation from the growing acceptance of a common financial reporting language. Capital markets have gone global and Canada accounts for less than 4% of the global capital markets. If every country speaks a different accounting language, investors have difficulty comparing companies and investors ultimately bear the costs of translation. A global accounting language is the best solution for both public companies and investors.

He added,

IFRS has been evaluated by the International Organization of Securities Commissions, including the SEC. The consensus is that the standards are comprehensive, robust and capable of consistent interpretation and application. The balance of informed opinion worldwide, including the United States and Canada, is that IFRS strikes the appropriate balance between fundamental principles and more specific implementation guidance.[3]

The Canadian Institute of Chartered Accountants (CICA) says,

The AcSB is adopting IFRS for publicly accountable enterprises to help them remain competitive within global capital markets. Not only will the adoption of IFRS improve the clarity and comparability of financial information globally; ultimately it will also prove more efficient and cost effective by eliminating the need for reconciliation of information reported under separate national standards.[4]

The term "publicly accountable" is based on the IFRS literature. The IFRS for private business distinguishes between publicly accountable entities for which full IFRS are the appropriate comprehensive basis of accounting, and nonpublicly accountable entities for which the IFRS for private business is available. Any company that issues securities in a public market is considered publicly accountable, as is any business that operates in a fiduciary capacity, such as a bank or insurance company. IFRS will apply to some 4,500 Canadian companies that have listed securities. The IFRS for private business also foresees the possibility that size may make a private company publicly accountable, but leaves this to national governments to determine since relative size depends on the nature of the national economy. The AcSB has decided that size will not be a basis for distinction for Canadian companies.

The AcSB, in its 2006 announcement, said that from that time it would start to take new IFRS into Canadian GAAP in order to reduce the impact of switchover. Of course, a number of new IFRS are joint standards that have been worked out with the FASB, and so U.S. companies are also in the position that their national GAAP is getting closer to IFRS over time.

For most Canadian companies, the actual switchover date will be January 1, 2010. They are only required to produce one year of comparative figures (as is the case in Europe) and so will have to produce only one year of parallel numbers. They will publish 2010 financial statements using Canadian GAAP but will subsequently have to publish a reconciliation between their Canadian GAAP figures and IFRS for that year. They will also have to provide 2010 comparative figures alongside the 2011 financials. Consequently, they will need to be in a position to construct an IFRS balance sheet for January 1, 2010.

When the EU moved to IFRS in 2005, the SEC, exceptionally, waived the requirement for 2 years of comparative data on first-time adoption of IFRS. EU companies registered with the SEC therefore had only to produce 2004 data under parallel accounting. This relaxation should also be available for Canadian adopters.

Unlike the United States, the Canadian authorities considered whether companies should be preparing for IFRS beginning with the initial 2006 announcement rather than waiting for the confirmation that was given in February 2008. CICA organizes regular surveys of readiness. At the end of 2008, their survey showed the results in Table 3.1.

A particular issue for the Canadian standard-setter was to identify early on in the process the possible technical problems that might be faced by Canadian companies. As they note, the impact will vary considerably from one company to another, and so it was essential for companies to look at their own situation early and identify what the issues would be. The standard-setter did a great deal of work in 2006 and 2007 to review the problems that the adopting companies would face. It considered these issues and then went to the IASB with requests to provide transitional relief at the changeover.

One such problem was that Canadian oil and gas companies using full cost accounting identified that they would have difficulty arriving at valuations of their oil reserves under IFRS. In principle, IFRS 1 *First-Time Adoption of IFRS* requires that when companies switch to the international standards, they must restate all prior balances to what they

*Table 3.1. Canadian Companies' Readiness Status*

| Goal | % |
| --- | --- |
| In process of assessing potential impact | 44 |
| Aware of changes, not begun to assess impact | 22 |
| Assessed impact, begun educating staff on changes | 12 |
| Started conversion process but not completed it | 6 |
| Completed education planning conversion | 5 |
| Have completed conversion process | 4 |
| Appointed a transition leader/team | 4 |
| Not aware of the upcoming changes | 2 |

*Source*: CICA/RBC Business Monitor (2008, Q4), p. 19.

would have been had IFRS been followed throughout. This retrospective restatement is, however, impossible to perform in many circumstances. Often companies do not retain original vouchers and other documentation beyond the previous 7 to 10 years, so going back to past acquisitions or past exploration is not possible. Even if such documentation has been maintained, recreating the accounting would be extremely difficult. Consequently, IFRS 1 offers a range of alternative solutions to deal with these situations. One of these is that fair value at the date of adoption can be used as "deemed cost" instead of restating historical cost.

However, the AcSB realized that this was going to be difficult to use because Canadian oil fields tend to be small and so companies have not historically disaggregated figures to individual properties. They use full cost accounting that is aggregated in large pools, often at a countrywide level. There is no historical cost data available at the level of the individual deposit (the cash generating unit under IFRS) and getting fair values would be a logistical nightmare given the large number of fields and the small number of professional valuers.[5]

The AcSB therefore went to the IASB with the problem and succeeded in getting the IASB to propose amendments to IFRS 1 to give relief. The IASB agreed to allow them to allocate the historical cost pools across properties. A similar proposal was also put to the IASB, and has been exposed, regarding accounting for activities subject to rate-regulation. Both of these proposals will be of particular use to U.S. companies in these circumstances. They would not have been able to do this had both the AcSB and the Canadian companies not gone down into the detail at a very early stage to see what the problems would be.

## Getting Ready for IFRS

The AcSB and CICA have gone to great lengths to try to ensure that the transition is as painless as possible. There is a major Internet resource at http://www.cica.ca/ifrs that is updated all the time. This includes publications, such as *The CICA's Guide to IFRS in Canada*, that discuss the impact of transition and also provides a checklist that compares IFRS to Canadian GAAP. The AcSB also has a number of useful documents,[6] including its IFRS implementation plan, bulletins summarizing key aspects of the plan, and analysis of the changes expected to IFRS before 2011.

The CICA has also published *20 Questions Directors and Audit Committees Should Ask About IFRS Conversions* by Rafik Greiss and Simon Sharp. They say,

> Converting to IFRS will not merely be a technical accounting exercise but more a widespread change management exercise that will impact many areas of the business. Any business function required to prepare financial information, or impacted by financial information, has the potential for change. Given the expected change in earnings and financial position, one should expect changes to
>
> - executive and employee evaluation and compensation plans;
> - foreign exchange and hedging activities;
> - corporate income taxes;
> - ratios and bank covenants;
> - internal controls and processes;
> - investor relations and communications to capital markets;
> - management reporting;
> - IT and data systems.[7]

The authors identify 10 "key areas that need to be addressed during the conversion" that provide a very useful starting point for company managers.[8]

1. *Project launch and planning activities.* The authors recommend that a project management team be established as soon as possible. Its first job would be an impact assessment that will identify the issues for the company and enable a plan to be drawn up and resources to be allocated. They state, "Any GAAP conversion project should commence with some form of impact assessment, diagnostic activity or scoping exercise."[9] They say all key managers should be aware of the plan and regular reports should be provided to monitor progress.

2. *Revision of accounting policies.* The authors point out that reassessing the company's accounting policies is a key to assessing what needs to

be done during the conversion phase. The accounting changes will drive shifts in performance measurement as well as possible IT systems changes and internal controls. The extent of these changes will impact staff training.

3. *Application of IFRS 1*. IFRS 1 has a number of options that companies can use to reduce the costs of change, but once these choices have been made, the company must live with them thereafter. The restatement rolls into a one-line adjustment of retained earnings. This is a good moment to review any preexisting problem areas and address them.

4. *Development of skeleton financial statements compliant with IFRS*. The authors see this as another exercise that will have impact on other areas. They recommend that companies look at their current disclosures and see how these will change under IFRS. This will help in advising analysts and other users as to how the statements will look and will help with data capture issues.

5. *Preparation of data under parallel accounting*. Most Canadian companies will have to prepare figures under both sets of GAAP for 1 year. Greiss and Sharp say this could be one of the most challenging areas of the project; therefore, management needs a clearly worked out approach.

6. *Transition approach*. The authors point out that there is a decision to make as to whether subsidiaries will switch to IFRS or whether conversion will be done only at the level of the group consolidation. They recommend that "accounting and controls should be pushed down to transaction level." They do not mention this, but where the group has foreign subsidiaries for whom IFRS are a possible basis of accounting, there are cost savings to be made in having all on the same basis as domestic subsidiaries.

7. *Identifying and resolving data capture issues*. To the extent that IFRS require additional or different data from Canadian GAAP, management are recommended to identify what data are needed so that it can be captured or analyzed in order to feed disclosure and, possibly, to modify IT systems.

8. *Retraining of personnel*. Management need to ensure that adequate training is given to personnel so that they have the knowledge to

ensure a smooth roll-out. Training is needed not only for accounting staff directly involved in processing but also for everyone in the group that uses financial statements in any way. The authors point out that the experience in Europe showed that there is competition for key personnel as changeover approaches and companies need to be sure they have defensive strategies for retaining staff.

9. *Communication with stakeholders.* According to Greiss and Sharp, "Managing investors' and other stakeholders' expectations with respect to the impacts of IFRS and the company's progress toward conversion will be an important area for boards to monitor. Clear, continuous and consistent communication with stakeholders will reduce the risk of misunderstandings and aid a smooth transition."

10. *Audit committee financial literacy and retraining.* Greiss and Sharp point out that the audit committee will need to be sufficiently well informed to be able to make a judgment on the appropriateness of management's decisions with respect to conversion. This means that they too will require adequate training early in the process.[10]

To assist financial statement users in becoming ready for IFRS, the organization of Canadian Securities Administrators (CSA) has specified the required disclosures in Management Discussion and Analysis in the periods leading up to the changeover.[11] These include increasing amounts of information about a company's plans for the changeover and the expected effects on its financial statements. The CICA has also published a guide, "Pre-2011 Communications About IFRS Conversion," that provides additional guidance in applying the CSA requirements.

## Conclusion

The Canadian conversion to IFRS provides a very convenient pilot exercise for the United States. Companies will be able to monitor the progress of their neighbors to the north and benefit from the experience when the United States switches—if it does—to IFRS in 2014.

There are a number of differences between the Canadian approach and that of the United States. Canada decided on a 5-year run-in, with an initial announcement in 2006, followed by confirmation in 2008, and conversion in 2011. The United States made its initial announcement in

2008 with confirmation to be made in 2011. However, whereas Canada said that confirmation was as good as certain and proceeded to take steps immediately to prepare for conversion, the United States is not prejudging the decision, so it is less clear to companies that it is worth investing a great deal into transition preparation prior to 2011. Nonetheless, accelerated filers for whom conversion could be in 2014 will have to be running dual accounting from 2012, just months after the SEC decision. They will need to have made a detailed impact assessment well before then.

Canada's long run-in under conditions of near certainty has meant that the Canadian standard-setter had time to assess the impact of transition on individual companies and then negotiate a modification of the first-time adoption IFRS.

Canada planned a "big bang" approach to conversion, as had been the case in Europe—except that they also provided for voluntary early adoption. The SEC, on the other hand, has preferred a staggered approach in the proposals that are out for comment. Those companies whose sector is dominated by IFRS reporting could apply for early adoption and in so doing will provide a pilot exercise for others. All other SEC registrants would switch over a 3-year period. The largest companies will move in 2014, the next in 2015, and the smallest in 2016. This means that investors would be faced with both U.S. GAAP and IFRS in the market at the same time. The big bang approach means that not only is there uniformity after conversion but also some doubts from users about interpretation of the data. The U.S. approach will force users to check which basis of accounting is being used but may familiarize them more gradually with the interpretation of IFRS statements.

# CHAPTER 4

# Major Technical Differences

In this chapter we are going to review a series of financial reporting issues in order to give some idea as to the similarities and differences between IFRS and U.S. GAAP. This is not intended to be an exhaustive list, and readers looking for a detailed analysis should go to a publication such as KPMG's *IFRS Compared to U.S. GAAP*[1] or PricewaterhouseCoopers' *Similarities and Differences—A Comparison of IFRS and US GAAP*.[2]

A problem faced by all authors compiling such analyses is that the subject is a moving target. Between 2009 and 2011, the IASB and the FASB have a program of further convergence. This should lead to converged standards on liabilities and equity, revenue recognition, financial statement presentation, and financial instruments. The IASB should complete work on its own standard on fair value measurement as well as a new standard on consolidation and special purpose entities and an amendment to its pensions' standard. The approach in this chapter will be to look at the situation in 2009 and indicate where it could be by 2011 when the IFRS decision is scheduled to be made by the SEC.

A generic issue as between IFRS and U.S. GAAP is that American standards are generally written to include much more detail and many more specificities than are IFRS. Companies that use IFRS tend, as a consequence, to rely on the support material prepared by academics and practitioners to provide practice information and make analogies. The Big Four international audit firms prepare application manuals. Ernst & Young, for example, produce *International GAAP*, published by John Wiley & Sons, and KPMG produce *Insights Into IFRS*, published by Thomson. One of the effects of the movement to a single worldwide standard has been that whereas national offices previously supplied technical leadership, the international firms now have a global technical structure for IFRS to try to ensure comparable application worldwide.

Another generic difference is that IFRS always ignore national legal requirements. Since the standards are not designed for individual jurisdictions, they leave aside specificities. This is one of the reasons that national standard-setters remain operational in jurisdictions where IFRS have been adopted—they may need to provide local guidance on how to apply IFRS in the context of local legal issues. This sometimes gives rise to difficulties, for example, when trying to converge IAS 12 *Income Taxes* with U.S. GAAP; it became clear that there are very different practices on recognition of an expected change of tax rate because of the different national legal structure. For example, in the United Kingdom, once the minister of finance has formally announced the government's intentions for the next tax year, these rates are routinely taken as final before the legislation has even been debated by Parliament. However, in the United States, no future rate is taken as final until the president has signed the legislation.

IAS 8 *Accounting Policies* includes a hierarchy for selecting an accounting policy when none is immediately found in a standard. This suggests that the first step is to analogize the policy to another standard or IFRIC Interpretation. If this does not yield a result, the preparer should look to the conceptual framework. Finally, the preparer could look to accounting standards issued by a national standard-setter that uses the same or a similar conceptual framework.

There are two points notable for U.S. companies. The FASB conceptual framework is written with the object of informing decisions by standard-setters and does not appear in the FASB Codification of GAAP. It is only to be considered when the preparer has exhausted the authoritative guidance in the Codification; under IFRS it is to be applied directly by the preparer before going outside the IASB literature.

The second point is that a U.S. company that fails to find a solution to a particular problem within the IASB literature can then, quite correctly, go to U.S. GAAP. One area where this is likely to be important is industry-specific guidance. The IASB has some minimal requirements for insurance companies and mineral extraction companies but is working on standards for these that will not surface until well after 2011. Outside of that, there are no sector-specific standards, and companies will likely fall back on U.S. GAAP for other issues. Indeed, revising industry-specific standards to converge with IFRS is one of the things that will probably keep the FASB busy for years if the SEC moves to IFRS.

# Financial Statement Presentation

The FASB and IASB have been working together for a few years on a project to revise and converge financial statement presentation. The first publication on this was a preliminary views discussion paper that came out in October 2008. *Preliminary Views on Financial Statement Presentation* sets out to make each of the financial statements fit cohesively with each other. It aims to have each statement have sections on operations, investment, and financing. All statements would be split into business and financing, and the business section would be further split between operations and investing. The exact split would be determined by preparers. Initial reactions to the proposals have been that the resulting statements are very complex. It remains to be seen how much of the original proposal will survive, but the aim is to complete the proposal by 2011, and so companies will likely be using that format under U.S. GAAP anyway.

Before then, the IFRS approach to presentation (to be found in IAS 1) does not *necessarily* give rise to financial statements different to those a U.S. company would issue. The IASB has followed the United States in requiring companies to prepare a "Statement of Comprehensive Income." (Prior to 2009 this was a presentational option only, and the statement including Other Comprehensive Income [OCI] was called the Statement of Recognized Income and Expense.) There was, however, much opposition to this, and the IASB agreed that companies could, if they wished, put regular earnings on one page, and then carry forward the subtotal to the next page where OCI is added to get to Total Comprehensive Income. The preliminary views paper also proposes keeping OCI items separate from operations. The project staff originally suggested OCI items should be integrated, but both standards' boards considered that it was still too radical a step to take. Corporations continue to be concerned about how analysts treat OCI data.

At a more detailed level, the balance sheet (the IASB now also uses "Statement of Financial Position") should be split between current and noncurrent items, depending on whether an item is part of the business cycle. However, IAS 1 does not prohibit a presentation based on liquidity if that is thought to give better information. Expenses may be shown by nature or by function. Historically, continental European companies used a presentation of expenses by nature (employment costs, depreciation and amortization, external supplies, etc.). However, most companies using IFRS use a presentation by function (cost of sales, marketing, and administration), although financial income and expense is separated. IFRS companies have to provide a statement of changes in equity.

The cash flow statement (IAS 7) has the same headings as its U.S. counterpart (and indeed was the first standard to be accepted by the SEC as equivalent to U.S. GAAP). However, as you might expect, it provides less detail about what goes into each heading than does the U.S. literature.

## Consolidation and Special Purpose Entities (SPEs)

This is likely to be an area where U.S. companies could find themselves consolidating more companies in which they have investments than they did previously. At present there is a fundamental difference between U.S. GAAP and IFRS on the scope of consolidation. The U.S. requirement, Accounting Research Bulletin (ARB) No. 51, talks about the parent usually having "a controlling financial interest," and U.S. practice is to look for ownership of the majority of voting shares in another company for that company to be included in the consolidated accounts. However, IAS 27 *Consolidated Financial Statements*, the substantive international standard in 2009, takes a broader view.

It says that an investee company should be consolidated when it is controlled by the parent. Control arises in any of the following situations: if the parent (a) owns 50% or more of the voting shares, (b) has the power to govern the financial and operating policies of the investee, (c) can appoint or remove the majority of the board of directors, or (d) can cast the majority of votes at the board meetings of the investee. However, in uncertain situations, control is a matter of fact, not of relationship. This could mean, for example, that if Company A owns 40% of the shares in Company B, and there are no other large blocks of shares in Company B, Company A would be deemed to have control and should consolidate Company B under IAS 27 where it would not under ARB No. 51.

In fact, the IASB is in the process of writing a new consolidation standard whereas the FASB is still hesitant on this issue. The official FASB position is that it has consolidations on its research agenda (i.e., not on its active agenda) and will review that position in light of the progress of the IASB project. The question was discussed in October 2008 at a joint meeting of the two standard-setting boards in Norwalk, Connecticut. On the one hand, the IASB was reluctant to issue its standard and then be obliged to amend it shortly afterward. On the other hand, the FASB would have to expose the elements in the IASB proposal that were different from the United States and redebate them. It is extremely unlikely that a converged standard will emerge by 2011.

A central issue is that the IASB's proposed new standard addresses off-balance sheet (OBS) vehicles as well as standard consolidation issues. The FASB has been working extensively on this area ever since Enron and is continuing to revise FIN 46(R), its main literature on the subject. It would rather reach a new version of that standard and then look at basic consolidation, while the IASB is doing the two together. On top of that, the FASB has its concept of the "variable interest entity" (VIE), which is based on what the standard-setters call a "risks and rewards" model. That is to say it is looking for consolidation by the entity that has most to gain and most at risk in the VIE.

The IASB's project staff favor maintaining the "control" model (i.e., one based on who is actually managing the entity). They note that the FIN 46(R) model provides structuring opportunities through a complex web of contractual rights that make it very difficult to see who is the main beneficiary. They consider that there is too much emphasis on the consolidation decision: there should be a category of relationships where supplementary disclosure is used to inform investors of the links between the entity and the group. Thus, the IASB project mentions "structured entities" and suggests that the accounting policy notes disclose why these have not been consolidated. This is backed up by disclosures as to the extent of the parent's activities in this area and the parent's continuing relationship with them.

The IASB literature pertaining to OBS vehicles that is still in force as of 2009 is SIC 12 *Consolidation—Special Purposes Entities*. This is a short interpretation that says a SPE should be consolidated when the substance of a relationship between the entity and the SPE indicates that the entity controls the SPE. This interpretation gives examples about the SPE acting for the entity or the entity receiving benefits. The IASB is not aware of any particular problems with the SIC, but it has a standing policy to incorporate new interpretations into the standard they are interpreting whenever that standard is open for amendment. At the same time, the Financial Stability Forum and the IOSC have both issued reports on the credit crisis during 2008 that called for a review of OBS entities and better disclosures. An exposure draft issued at the end of 2008 was intended to lead to a replacement standard for IAS 27 that will also cover SPEs. This will be in force by 2011, but it is too early in its evolution to be worth analyzing at this time.

To sum up, U.S. companies can expect a switch to an approach that requires the exercise of judgment as to whether another company is controlled or not. The level of investment in the equity of that company will not be the sole determining factor. As far as OBS vehicles are concerned, the credit crisis has placed a spotlight on these and it is certain disclosures will be expanded. However, it is impossible to predict where either the FASB or IASB will be by 2011.

By contrast, the IASB's business combinations standard, IFRS 3, was issued to catch up with the FASB and subsequently revised as a joint project with the FASB. That said, there are some differences, notably on impairment, which is dealt with later.

## Revenue Recognition

Revenue recognition is covered in one general standard, IAS 18 *Revenue*, but there are specific issues dealt with in IAS 11 *Construction Contracts*, as well as IAS 41 *Agriculture*, IAS 17 *Leases*, IAS 39 *Financial Instruments*, and a number of interpretations. IAS 18 calls for revenue to be recognized when the following occur:

1. The entity has transferred the significant risks and rewards of ownership of the goods to the buyer
2. The entity retains neither continuing managerial involvement to the degree usually associated with ownership nor effective control over the goods sold
3. The amount of revenue can be measured reliably
4. It is probable that the economic benefits associated with the transaction will flow to the entity
5. The costs incurred or to be incurred in respect of the transaction can be measured reliably

This is comparable with Staff Accounting Bulletin (SAB) 104.

The staff believes that revenue generally is realized or realizable and earned when all of the following criteria are met:

1. Persuasive evidence of an arrangement exists.
2. Delivery has occurred or services have been rendered.
3. The seller's price to the buyer is fixed or determinable.
4. Collectibility is reasonably assured.

However, the U.S. literature is much more extensive in respect to individual industries, and as argued above, in the absence of IFRS literature, a company would likely be able to use U.S. GAAP.

IAS 11 requires a percentage of completion to be used on construction contracts and prohibits recognition only on completion. This is broadly similar to the U.S. practice, although the completed contract method is possible in some situations.

Revenue recognition is a subject that has been on the joint agenda of the IASB and FASB for some years, but has been put on the list of new joint standards to be completed for 2011. After looking at a number of more or less exotic choices for addressing recognition under a contract for multiple deliverables, a joint discussion paper issued in 2008 settles for the traditional approach. A proportion of the contract price is recognized when a deliverable is completed.

A number of board members favored moving to an approach where the entity recognizes an asset (the price the customer is to pay) and a liability (the cost of satisfying the customer) at the point that a firm contract is agreed. The effect of such an approach would have been to cause a "selling profit" to be recognized when the contract is agreed, rather than when the goods or services are delivered. Some people liked this because it recognized two different activities (selling and providing the good or service) as having different risks and returns, and it also caused executory contracts to come within the financial statements. At present, the existence of most unfulfilled contracts (executory contracts) is ignored by the financial reporting system even though in some industries it is a significant piece of information.

However, this proposal ran into opposition because other people with more conservative instincts found recognition of some profit at inception unacceptable and considered that the allocation between the selling and supplying activities provided an opportunity for manipulation. It would have involved a significant shift in the timing of recognition.

The new standard will probably provide a new analytical framework for considering revenue recognition decisions. The focus will be on determining whether a new asset or liability has been created. In practice, however, it is likely to have little effect on timing of recognition or measurement in most cases. It may impact the timing of recognition for long-term contracts where no deliverables are completed during the fulfillment of the contract.

# Nonfinancial Assets

There are a number of differences between U.S. GAAP and IFRS. In particular IFRS require capitalization of development costs; allow property, plant, and equipment to be held at valuation; and allow investment property to be measured at fair value on a continuing basis. However, in practice, these differences are likely to affect only a small number of industries.

Accounting for intangible assets is addressed by IAS 38. This includes goodwill and research and development. Goodwill must be allocated to individual cash-generating units (CGUs), or groups of CGUs that cannot exceed a segment. Under U.S. GAAP, goodwill is allocated to that segment or one level below. Under both sets of GAAP, goodwill is no longer amortized but must be tested annually for impairment. Commentators consider that allocation of goodwill under IFRS is typical to lower levels of activity, and impairment is therefore recognized more frequently.

A significant difference between IFRS and U.S. GAAP is in the treatment of research and development costs. SFAS 2 *Accounting for Research and Development Costs* requires that research and development costs are expensed as incurred, with an annual disclosure as to the amount. IAS 38 requires that research costs are expensed but development costs must be capitalized provided that the entity considers that they are recoverable and the development will lead to a commercially feasible outcome that the entity is able to exploit. Evidently the dividing line between the pure research phase and the development of a commercial product or process is difficult to assess and is another example of the need for judgment on the part of the entity and its auditors, a judgment that is inherent in IFRS.

IAS 38 has both a cost model and a revaluation model. Under the cost model, intangibles are amortized over their expected economic life. Where they have an indefinite life, they are not amortized but are tested for impairment. While the standard allows for the possibility to hold an intangible at valuation, it also states that this is only possible where there is an active market for this type of intangible. This paragraph adds that such markets are rare because of the individual nature of most intangibles and *cannot exist* for "brands, newspaper mastheads, music and film publishing rights, patents or trademarks, because each such asset is unique."[3]

The standard does not permit the recognition of internally generated intangibles. Both the IASB and FASB accept that it is inconsistent to recognize all intangibles, including those generated internally—that is, those acquired in a business combination—while not recognizing any other internally generated intangibles. They had on their 2008 Memorandum of Understanding a milestone to consider internally generated intangibles. A research paper was prepared by the staff of the Australian Accounting Standards Board (AASB), but at the end of 2007 the IASB and FASB decided that the subject was not sufficiently urgent to be given time on their current active agenda and it remains on their research agenda.

The AASB published a discussion paper in November 2008 to try to keep the subject alive. The paper advances two approaches. Under one, only planned intangibles would be recognized. The accounting would follow a cost accumulation model once a plan to create an asset had been agreed. Under the other, assets could be recognized retrospectively, but the original costs may not have been distinguished and would already have passed into earnings.

The standard on property, plant, and equipment (IAS 16) is broadly similar to the U.S. requirements. All the costs of bringing an asset into service should be capitalized. Under IFRS this includes interest costs (but this is not calculated in the same way as under U.S. GAAP) and possible hedging gains and losses (excluded in the United States). The standard also envisages both cost and valuation models. Where property is held at valuation, the carrying value must be reassessed at regular intervals. In practice this option is used infrequently.

IAS 16 requires a component approach to recognition and depreciation. Related assets with different useful lives should be recognized and depreciated independently. So a heating plant within an office building would be held separately from the building—this is allowed but not required in the United States. Decommissioning provisions are created by increasing the carrying value of the asset to be decommissioned and are amortized with the asset, as under U.S. GAAP.

However, the treatment of investment property is substantially different under IFRS. Under U.S. GAAP there is no distinction made for this kind of property, and it is accounted for at cost under general property, plant, and equipment rules. IAS 40 *Investment Property* identifies this special class as

> property (land or a building—or part of a building—or both) held (by the owner or by the lessee under a finance lease) to earn rentals or for capital appreciation or both, rather than for: (a) use in the production or supply of goods or services or for administrative purposes; or (b) sale in the ordinary course of business.

Such property is recognized initially at cost, but subsequent measurement may be under the cost model or using fair value. Under the latter, the property is carried at its market price at the balance sheet date.

The IASB put in place a standard (IFRS 5) to converge its treatment of assets held for sale with that of the FASB. Once an asset or disposal group is identified as held for sale, it is carried at fair value less costs to sell and is no longer depreciated. It is disclosed separately in the financial statements.

## Impairment

Impairment is an area where U.S. GAAP and IFRS have more or less the same underlying principle but differ on a great many details. There are no plans for convergence in this area yet. Under IAS 36, the CGU is the smallest group of assets that has cash inflows largely independent of the rest of the group. Under U.S. GAAP, the CGU is at reporting-unit level, which is one level below segment. Goodwill and intangibles with indefinite lives have to be tested annually for impairment under both sets of standards. For other assets there has to be some indication of possible impairment to require a test.

Under IFRS, a CGU is impaired if its carrying amount is higher than its "recoverable amount." The recoverable amount in this case is the higher of the fair value less costs to sell, or the "value in use." Value in use is the net present value of the CGU's expected future cash flows. Value in use is based on entity-specific cash flows discounted at a rate that reflects the risk of the asset being measured. When a CGU is deemed to be impaired, the impairment is charged against the goodwill in the first case, and then to other assets. The write-off of goodwill cannot be reversed, but that of other assets may be.

U.S. GAAP prefers to measure individual assets (other than goodwill) for impairment, rather than groups of assets. The U.S. approach works in two steps. First, the asset is tested to see if it is impaired—that is, whether the carrying value exceeds the undiscounted expected future cash flows (also known as the recoverable amount). If the asset fails the test, U.S. GAAP then has a separate measurement of the actual impairment. The asset is restated to its fair value. Impairment write-offs cannot be reversed.

On the face of it, the IFRS impairment approach would be likely to lead to identification of more impairments than would be the case under U.S. GAAP. In the first place, the CGU is generally smaller, thus limiting the possibility of more profitable units obscuring less profitable units. In the second place, the U.S. hurdle to a recoverable amount is higher than IFRS because it is undiscounted.

## Financial Instruments

Both the IASB and the FASB believe that the only long-term solution to financial instruments is to measure all of them at fair value (see, e.g., IASB discussion paper *Reducing Complexity in Reporting Financial Instruments*). As David Tweedie remarks, IAS 39—the financial instrument measurement standard—should be one page: measure everything at fair value. The reason it runs to over 300 pages (and the U.S. literature is contained in so many different statements, etc.) is all the exceptions it must list.

Accounting for financial instruments as currently mandated is extremely complex under both bases of accounting. The chief financial officer of an Anglo-Swedish company, AstraZeneca, faced with applying

IAS 39 from 2005 onward, decided that the group did not really need to use derivatives. It got rid of its financial instruments so it did not need to use IAS 39. No doubt many European banks would have liked to follow suit more recently. Both U.S. GAAP and IFRS have a similar approach to accounting for financial instruments, but at the detailed level there are many differences.

Under both sets of standards, debts, liabilities, and receivables are held at amortized cost and all derivatives are held at fair value. However, under IFRS all financial instruments have to be classified at inception as

- available for sale,
- held for trading , and
- held to maturity.

However, the IASB also gives companies the option of classifying instruments at fair value through profit and loss if the company manages the instruments on a fair value basis or to correct an asset-liability mismatch. This is narrower than the fair value option available under U.S. GAAP—even if the U.S. option was given in the spirit of convergence. Held-for-trading securities are automatically valued at fair value through profit and loss whereas available-for-sale securities are held at fair value through OCI. Held-to-maturity instruments are carried at amortized cost.

In theory, instruments are classified at inception and all instruments of the same class must be classified similarly. However, the IASB did, in the context of the credit crisis, pass an amendment in 2008 to allow available-for-sale instruments to be reclassified in rare circumstances.

The impairment rules are slightly different. IFRS require that when objective evidence exists for an impairment, this should be recognized through profit and loss—even for available-for-sale instruments—but some impairment losses can be reversed. Under U.S. GAAP, the impairment has to be other than temporary to be recognized, but it is then not reversible. The approach to derecognition is also slightly different insofar as IAS 39 is based on a risks and rewards approach, while U.S. GAAP is based on control.

The one thing that we can be sure about is that by 2012 some of the details will have changed. There is currently a joint IASB/FASB team working on derecognition, and at the end of 2008 the boards decided to accelerate their project to improve their financial instruments standards.

The IASB issued its discussion paper *Reducing Complexity in Reporting Financial Instruments* in March 2008, and the paper was also issued that month by the FASB with their own call for comments. The intention at the time was to acknowledge that both boards saw the ultimate objective having all financial instruments reported at fair value. However, they accepted that the world was not ready for that step, but that the existing literature is too complicated. The discussion paper therefore set out a series of alternative intermediate steps that might be taken to simplify the accounting, short of going to full fair value.

During 2008, the standard-setters were under a lot of pressure to converge their standards on financial instruments and to improve them. As a consequence, they decided to accelerate the project while governments have exerted pressure to have a new, simplified standard in place by 2010. At the time of writing, it is too early to say whether this is a realistic proposition. On the face of it, financial institutions have been penalized by fair value during 2007 and 2008 and there would be not much appetite for extending its scope. Against that, when the IASB said in 2001 that it was going to issue a standard on employee stock options, the Financial Executives International (FEI) representative on the SAC warned them that corporations would fight them tooth and nail. However, the IASB standard and the FASB counterpart, SFAS 123(R), went through quickly and with relatively little opposition.

All we can say at the moment is that while the principles of the IFRS and U.S. literature are much the same, the detail has many differences. The situation will continue to evolve!

## Liabilities and Equity

The situation on the classification of liabilities and equity is similar to that of financial instruments generally: the underlying principles are much the same, but the United States has more detailed rules and the details are sometimes different. Under IFRS (IAS 32) an instrument that involves the entity in an obligation to settle for cash or any other financial instrument is treated as a liability, as would be the case in the United States.

However, the IASB has departed from this strict principle to address the problem of stock that is puttable back to the issuer. In some countries there are legal entities where stockholders are not allowed to sell their shares other than back to the entity. This is the case, apparently, for some German forms of limited liability partnerships and New Zealand farming cooperatives. Strict application of IAS 32 would mean that if the entity were profitable, the fair value of its instruments would rise—but as they were classified as liabilities this would involve recognition of a loss. The IASB created an exception. An obligation for an entity to buy back its own equity instruments is normally classified as a liability under IFRS, but this is not always the case in the United States either.

U.S. GAAP, on the other hand, has a mezzanine category between equity and liabilities into which instruments redeemable at the option of the holder, or those that would otherwise be categorized as equity, are displayed. Under IFRS, compound financial instruments have to be bifurcated. Minority interests are shown under IFRS as a separate category within group equity, whereas in the United States they are in the mezzanine.

Companies that have to start maintaining IFRS data in 2012 can be sure they will face a change. However, this too is an area that is being worked on by the standard-setters. The FASB has had a project running for a number of years on classification of liabilities and equity. A paper on preliminary views was issued by the FASB in 2007 and subsequently also by the IASB. The intention is that a new joint standard should be issued by 2011. It is unlikely that this will be radically different from current practice, but given the wish to converge, both U.S. and IFRS approaches can expect some movement on the detail.

## Provisions and Contingencies

This is an area where the IASB and FASB use slightly different vocabulary. For the IASB a "provision" is a contingency for which an accrual is made (i.e., what appears in the financial statements as an expense and a liability). A "contingent liability" is a contingency for which a disclosure is made in the footnotes. The substantive standard under IFRS is IAS 37, and under U.S. GAAP it is SFAS 5, as subsequently amended in a number of pronouncements.

The likelihood of recognition of a liability of this kind is theoretically higher under IFRS than under U.S. GAAP because the threshold under IFRS is lower. For IAS 37, a provision is created when there is a legal or constructive obligation arising from a past event from which there will be a probable future outflow of resources that can be estimated reliably. Under IFRS, the "probable" threshold is more than 50% likely. For SFAS 5, the likelihood of there being a liability is also probable—but this means about 80% likely. U.S. GAAP does not automatically accrue for constructive obligations, and this is mandated in particular situations only.

Under IFRS, a contingent liability is a possible obligation whose existence will be confirmed only by a future event or where the outflow is unlikely or cannot be estimated with sufficient reliability. Companies using IFRS generally report litigation that is in process under the contingent liability footnote.

However, this position is supposed to change. The IASB has been working on amending IAS 37 for some time, and a new version of the standard should be in place by 2010. This new version will be different in two main respects. First, it will align IAS 37 with SFAS 146 on accounting for termination of businesses. Second, it will abandon the notion of the contingent liability and contingent asset. The IASB's analysis is that all contingent liabilities consist of an actual liability and an uncertainty. For example, if a company receives a legal complaint, it immediately has a liability to incur costs to address that, irrespective of the merit of the complaint.

The IASB argues that IAS 37 has an artificial threshold—a claim that is 49% likely to succeed is not recognized, but one that is 51% likely to succeed would be recognized. They are therefore moving to a position where all contingencies contain certain liabilities that must be recognized, and the uncertainty is built into the measurement. For example, a claim for compensation for injury by an employee for $10 million that the entity considers has a 30% chance of succeeding would be recognized as a liability for $3 million. A significant difference to U.S. practice is that this approach should also apply to litigation contingencies. The 2010 revision of IAS 37 will likely specify that the expected value of litigation claims should be recognized. IASB staff believe that preparers assert that it is impractical to do this.

Overall, it is likely that more provisions would be recognized under the current IAS 37 than under the U.S. literature, and when the standard changes, the difference would theoretically be greater, although the probability remains a management estimate. The name of the standard will also change. It will become IAS 37 *Liabilities*.

## Pensions

Accounting for pensions and related postemployment costs is, of course, a potentially major element of an entity's financial position and can impact investor perceptions strongly. Here again is an area where the underlying fundamentals are broadly the same under both systems, but the detail can be very different. There is a further complication here in that the two standard-setters have signed up to a joint project to create a new standard, but this is unlikely to be in force before 2014 at the earliest. This would mean that large accelerated filers would have to work with IAS 19 *Employee Benefits* in 2012 and switch to the new standard later.

Historically, the IASB has always tried to avoid having new adopters switch systems twice in a short period. When Europe adopted in 2005, the IASB agreed on a 4-year standstill where no changes would be obligatory. Its present 2011 targets for standard setting have that deadline because of the significant second wave of adopters coming in at that time. The likelihood is that the following set of targets would have a 2014 deadline if the United States decided to proceed in line with the SEC's present roadmap.

This would mean that either they would have to accelerate work on the new pensions' standard so that it could be implemented in 2014, or defer it until about 2017. However, if they did defer it, this would create the double-change scenario. To avoid that, it is just as possible that they could change the first-time adoption rules to suspend IAS 19 for U.S. adopters

As it presently stands, IAS 19 does not distinguish between postemployment benefits and postretirement benefits, and neither does it have separate arrangements for pensions as opposed to other postemployment benefits. Like the U.S. literature, the standard distinguishes between the defined-benefit plan and the defined-contribution plan. Obligations under a defined-benefit plan are accrued during the employee's lifetime on the projected-unit credit method. While current year charges are taken to the income statement, changes in actuarial estimates can be recognized using a choice of three methods. They can be recognized in income, can be taken to OCI, or can be deferred using a corridor mechanism similar to what was originally available under GAAP.

A study of choices made by 523 European companies comprising the stock indices[4] showed that 232 used OCI, 256 used the corridor, and 35 went directly to income. However, if you remove the United Kingdom from the sample, it reduces to 377, with 86 using OCI and 257 using the corridor (the preexisting UK standard already mandated that treatment). Nonetheless, the IASB has indicated that it wishes to abandon the corridor. A 2008 discussion paper on that and other pension issues received quite a few comments supporting that idea. If U.S. adopters had to start keeping IAS 19 figures from 2012, they could assume that the corridor would have disappeared. In 2009 the IASB made a tentative decision to require all pension-related costs to flow through the income statement. This would be disaggregated to break out service costs and interest as the liability discount is unwound, as well as to allow for remeasurement. It remains to be seen whether this will make it through to a final amendment.

The treatment of multiemployer and group pension plans is also slightly different under IFRS. Under IAS 19, the individual employer must decide whether the plan is defined contribution or defined benefit in nature and follow the rules accordingly. Only if the information to compute the benefit obligation is not available can a defined-benefit plan be treated as defined contribution. Under U.S. GAAP, all such plans are treated as defined contribution.

It may be worth mentioning that under IFRS 1 *First-Time Adoption of IFRS*, a business moving to IAS 19 has to calculate the assets and liabilities of the defined-benefit plan under the international standard and any deficit that arises flows through to a one-time adjustment to retained earnings.

# Leasing

The IFRS requirements are contained in IAS 17 *Leases,* which is much the same as SFAS 13 *Accounting for Leases.* IAS 17 draws the distinction between a finance lease and an operating lease, as SFAS 13 does between a capital lease and an operating lease. The main difference between them is that IAS 17 defines a finance lease as one where the risks and rewards of using an asset have passed substantially to the lessee. This is a classic example of the difference between IFRS and U.S. standards. The American literature contains a series of quantitative measures to determine if a lease is a capital lease: the lease covers at least 75% of the useful life of the asset, or the present value of the rentals is more than 90% of the cost of the asset.

That said, standard-setters believe that the main effect of both these leasing standards was to cause the leasing industry to rewrite its leases so that they failed the finance-capital criteria. There is no evidence that one has produced better compliance than the other. David Tweedie is fond of remarking that he looks forward to the day when he can fly in an aircraft that also appears on the airline's balance sheet.

The IASB also has a corresponding interpretation, IFRIC 4 *Determining Whether an Arrangement Contains a Lease.* This states that some contracts can provide the use of an asset without being formally a leasing contract, and it contains guidance on assessing this and on appropriate accounting.

The IASB and FASB are working on a new joint leasing standard, and this is scheduled for completion by 2011. A discussion paper was issued in March 2009. This suggested abandoning the distinction between capital and operating leases and requiring that all leased assets should be recognized as assets in the balance sheet with a corresponding lease rental obligation. However, the proposal may seek to maintain a difference and recognize both as "right of use" assets or "in-substance purchased" assets. The lessee would be obliged to determine what was the likely useful life, irrespective of options in the lease term. The main aim is antiabuse, given the noncompliance with the substance of SFAS 13 and IAS 17. Leasing was one of the issues (along with pension obligations) identified by the SEC in their Sarbanes-Oxley-mandated study of OBS liabilities where major liabilities were not apparent.[5] The likelihood is that all SEC registrants will have to use this new standard from 2011 onward.

# Other Issues

IFRS 7 *Operating Segments* contains the IASB rules for segment reporting. This is the most obvious piece of convergence—the standard is virtually the same as SFAS 131, so U.S. companies will be familiar with it.

IFRS 2 *Share-Based Payment* addresses all transactions where the entity issues equity, or an equity option, instead of an asset in settlement of an obligation. Its main effect, however, is to require expensing of stock options granted to employees. In that area it is close to SFAS 123(R), which was developed alongside it. Both provide for recognition of the fair value of the option at grant date with truing up of the charge in the light of actual performance. Some commentators suggest that there is a slight difference in application that can impact the grant date. The IFRS refers to grant date being the point at which there is a "shared understanding" of the terms and conditions, whereas U.S. practice is to consider grant date to be the date the option is approved by shareholders, which could be some time later.

IAS 12 *Income Taxes* is another of these areas where the U.S. GAAP and IFRS approaches are the same but the detailed application can be different. Both standards base deferred tax provisions on the difference between the book carrying value of assets and liabilities and the tax carrying value. The IASB and FASB have been working to try to eliminate these differences as much as possible, but some are likely to remain—mostly because the U.S. literature naturally addresses the U.S. tax laws and their specificities, while the international standard sits outside any legal tax framework. The IASB will issue a revised standard before 2011, and the impact of difference is unlikely to be great in bottom-line terms. However, some costs may be generated for the staff tracking tax within the company.

IAS 34 *Interim Financial Reporting* addresses financial statements that cover part of the financial year (the IASB does not mandate the frequency of reporting, which is the prerogative of national government). The standard requires that the statements report data as if they covered a full reporting period, and they should be consistent with the annual financial statements. However, it does allow the use of condensed financial statements and does not require repetition of some elements that are available in the annual financial statements. SEC reporting requirements would override IAS 34 without being inconsistent in approach. IASB members think this is an unsatisfactory standard, but they do not yet have the time to overhaul it.

IAS 28 *Investment in Associates* addresses investments in other companies where the investor has "significant influence" ("equity investments" in the United States). This, as under U.S. GAAP, is the case where the investor has 20% or more of the voting stock but less than 50%. Equity accounting is used so that the change in net assets of the investee is reflected proportionately in the income statement of the investor. Generally speaking, standard-setters think equity accounting does not provide useful information. Many would prefer to see equity investments valued at fair value, but they have enough fires to fight at this time.

IAS 31 *Interests in Joint Ventures* bases its approach to these on the legal form used for the arrangement. Proportionate consolidation is an option, but this is scheduled to disappear. The IASB is working on a revised standard that would focus instead on the substance of the "joint arrangement" and require entities to account separately for assets that were managed in a joint arrangement or for their investment depending on the circumstances. The proposals have proved controversial, but a new standard should be in force for 2011. The United States favors the equity method.

IAS 10 *Events After the Reporting Date* deals with the treatment of information that becomes available after the balance sheet date but before the financial statements are finalized. Events that shed additional light on the situation at balance sheet date ("adjusting events") should be incorporated in the statements but not events that change that position subsequently. This is the same as U.S. GAAP except that under the international standard, where a loan covenant had been breached at balance sheet date and the problem has been resolved later, the breach should still be reported.

IAS 24 *Related Party Disclosures* addresses circumstances under which entities should provide details of transactions with management, owners, and so on. It also includes a requirement to disclose the remuneration of key management personnel.

IAS 41 *Agriculture* was originally produced at the instigation of the World Bank. Broadly, it requires that biological assets be measured at their fair value less costs to sell at balance sheet date. Practice has revealed some issues about how fair value is calculated. For example, should a 2-year-old plantation of trees be measured at what it could be sold for at 2 years old, or at a proportion of its expected price at maturity, adjusted for risk and discounted? The latter is the correct answer.

IFRS 6 *Exploration for and Evaluation of Mineral Resources* is a temporary holding standard that the IASB issued for the 2005 wave of adopters to allow them to continue to use their existing accounting. The central issue is that under existing IFRS an entity would not be permitted to recognize an exploration asset. The costs of prospecting and taking exploratory samples, drilling, and so on do not constitute an asset because there is no expectation of probable future cash inflows. This is an issue that has caused problems for U.S. standard-setters in the past, and the government has intervened. The IASB took the position that the issue was too complicated to address within the time available and so issued this holding standard.

The IASB has a task force from Canada, Australia, Norway, and South Africa working toward a new standard; they subsequently produced a discussion paper published in 2008 addressing mineral reserves. The team has worked with industry groups to bring definitions for oil and gas and those for mineral closer. It also suggests recognition of two other related assets: legal rights and information. They argue that the information gained from exploratory work can be sold, and so has expected future cash flows, and meets the definition of an asset. The project remains on the research agenda at the moment and will not result in a standard in the near future.

IFRS 4 *Insurance Contracts* is a similar standard in that its objective was to permit insurers to continue to use national rules until the IASB could provide a definitive standard. However, IFRS 4 still imposes some requirements on insurers. It includes a liability adequacy test and a requirement to separate deposits and embedded derivatives from insurance contracts. Catastrophe provisions are prohibited for new contracts. It also has disclosure requirements.

The IASB inherited a project on insurance contracts from its predecessor body, and this is considered to be the IASB's longest running project. It is set to beat IAS 39, which was the predecessor body's record 12 years. The IASB's view is that insurance companies have both insurance contracts and financial instrument contracts and should refer to the appropriate standard, rather than having a unique standard for insurance companies as is the case in the United States.

The IASB originally hoped to have its insurance standard finished by 2005, but it became clear that this was unlikely and IFRS 4 was issued as a holding standard. However, the standard-setter is currently aiming to have a final standard by 2011, and the FASB has issued its discussion paper. In the early part of the decade, there was substantial resistance from the insurance industry to the IASB's work. This resistance provided an opportunity for the arrival of the IASB's only professional lobbyist, Doug Barnert, who specializes in the insurance industry and the creation of industry groupings from North America, Europe, and Japan.

Over time, resistance has ebbed away somewhat, and the insurers have been drawn in to working on the project. It is now more or less acknowledged that there is a wide diversity of practices in accounting for insurance contracts around the world and that this is an unsatisfactory situation in the context of an industry where the largest players have a global reach.

The IASB project will impact some national practices more than others, but it will probably impact all insurance companies to some degree. However, there are several key issues that remain controversial, and it seems extremely unlikely that a final standard will emerge by 2011.

## Conclusion

This chapter has tried to point out the main similarities and differences between U.S. GAAP and IFRS so that U.S. managers can focus on these. However, it is often the case that the devil is in the detail, and it is therefore difficult to suggest how a standard affects individual companies without detailed knowledge of their transactions. Working out the probable impact on an individual company is a task that will need to be undertaken nearer the transition time and probably in conjunction with a specialist.

This chapter aims to provide the material for an initial assessment of where the most likely problem areas are in terms of IFRS transition. At the same time, it also points to the current work program of the two standard-setters with the object of forecasting where the position may have moved to by 2011 when the SEC expects to make its big IFRS decision.

# CHAPTER 5

# IASB's Standard-Setting Process

People who are used to dealing with the FASB will not find the operation of the IASB much different. The IASB might make greater use of discussion papers that state their preliminary views on a subject. Their exposure periods are longer as are their delays before implementation in order to give time for translations to be made and for standards to be incorporated in the law in jurisdictions where that is a requirement.

On major topics, the IASB holds roundtables in different parts of the world. Its board members travel the world frequently to have meetings with national standard-setters and constituents. Typically, the national standard-setter retains an important role after adoption of IFRS in terms of providing technical inputs to joint staff teams, liaising with their own constituents, and so on. It is virtually certain that the FASB would retain a key role in international standard setting if the SEC adopted IFRS. At the moment, the IASB is headquartered in the city of London, but it visits Norwalk, Connecticut, once a year for a joint meeting with the FASB. The FASB in turn also makes an annual visit to London.

On all major projects, the IASB aims to issue a preliminary views discussion paper, redeliberates in the light of comments, issues an exposure draft, further deliberates the responses, and issues a final standard. For companies affected by a proposed standard, it is vital to keep in touch with discussions at the preliminary views stage. When the IASB issues an exposure draft, it considers that it has looked at all the arguments put forward (in response to the preliminary views discussion paper), and it doesn't expect to change much, if anything, between the exposure draft and the final standard. Generally, the IASB does not like to reexpose and has only done so very rarely. Faced with doubt, the standard-setters tend to mandate the more rigorous choice in the exposure draft so that they can pull back a little if they feel that appropriate in the final standard.

Therefore, companies and institutions that want to influence the outcome of the debate need to do so at the preliminary views stage. European companies other than those in banking and insurance have largely not got that message yet, and they complain that the IASB does not listen when they object to a final standard. Of course, they needed to lobby 3 years earlier at least.

In this chapter we will set out the IASB's governance structure, its due process, and how to lobby it. The chapter will then look at the IFRIC and its processes and how national standard-setters interact with the international process.

## Organizational Structure

The keystone of the international standard-setter's structure is the IASC Foundation, a Delaware corporation whose trustees are tasked with raising money and appointing members of the IASB and its associated bodies. The overall structure at the beginning of 2009 is illustrated in Figure 5.1.

At the beginning of 2009, the trustees modified their constitution to create a further governing body, the Monitoring Board. This consists of representatives of the SEC, European Commission, Japanese Financial Services Agency, and the IOSCO. The Basel Committee on Banking

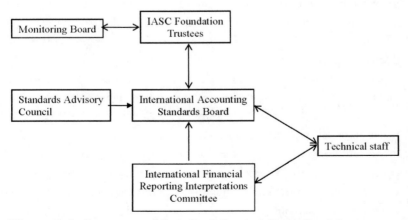

*Figure 5.1. Structure of Standard-Setting Organization*

Supervision is an observer member. The Monitoring Board will monitor the decisions made by the trustees of the IASC Foundation, but will have no direct input to the IASB.

This structure is intended to put the trustees in the position of protecting the standard-setting board from political or other interference. In some ways it has been too successful, and the European Commission has often complained that, although it represented the largest block of countries using IFRS, it has no control over or any input into the governance structure of the organization. There are 22 trustees, including a minimum of 6 from Europe, but they are not appointed by the commission. A few years ago the trustees created the Appointments Advisory Group to respond to the criticism that they were a self-perpetuating body: new trustees are appointed by the old trustees. But by 2009 the Appointments Group has disappeared, made redundant by the Monitoring Board, which has the right to comment on all decisions and to make suggestions. The Monitoring Board represents the bodies that regulate the major capital markets or those that mandate accounting in those markets.

The trustees carry out periodic reviews of their constitution every 5 years. The first review involved some fine-tuning, but the second review, currently in progress, will bring more significant changes. The Monitoring Board is an accelerated part of the second constitutional review. Other changes will take place as a result of the second review.

The funding of the IASC Foundation is considered to be controversial by some. Initially, individual companies, institutions, and audit firms contributed to its funding. Currently it still has a mixture of funding sources, although the trustees have been working toward agreeing on targets with individual countries and agreeing on a body in each country that is responsible for raising that money. In Germany, it is the German Accounting Standards Committee that coordinates funds, and in the United Kingdom, it is the Financial Reporting Council (a government body with financial reporting oversight). In France, an employer's organization has responsibility.

In 2007, the foundation's revenues were about $30 million (at 2007 exchange rates), of which just under a third was from selling publications; the rest was from donations. The Big Four audit firms each contributed

$1.5 million. The United Kingdom contributed about $1.5 million in total, Japan $2 million, and the United States $4 million.

The IASB has 14 members of whom 2 are part-time. The chairman is David Tweedie, whose past roles include being a technical partner at KPMG and a professor at the University of Edinburgh. In 1990 he was appointed chairman of the UK Accounting Standards Board, which he left in 2000 to take up his present post. His role includes that of chief executive of the IASC Foundation.

The IASB includes a number of American members. Jim Leisenring, a member of the FASB for 10 years, was a founding member. Dr. Mary Barth, of Stanford University, is a part-time member. John Smith, a financial instruments specialist from Deloitte, New York, was a part-time member until he retired from Deloitte and became a full-time member. Tony Cope, a financial analyst and former member of the FASB, was also a founding member and retired in 2007. Bob Herz, the current FASB chairman, was also a founding member of the IASB and served as a part-time member until he was nominated to the FASB in 2002. Prabhakar Kalavacherla, a partner in KPMG's San Francisco office, joined the board in 2009.

The original constitution required that board members should have "professional competence and practical experience," and the trustees enjoined to create "a group of people representing, within that group, the best available combination of technical expertise and diversity of international business and market experience."[1] The constitution says that geographical criteria should not apply, and no particular constituency or geographical interest shall dominate.

The predecessor board, however, *had* been based on geographical representation, and this was one of the most controversial issues in creating the new structure. It was eventually decided that the structure should be similar to the FASB, but even then with a board double the size of the FASB.

The initial board was dominated by Anglophone standard-setters. It included four Americans, one Canadian, four British, one South African, and one Australian. The other three members were French, Japanese, and Swiss. Some European commentators bemoaned the lack of European presence (preferring to think of Britain as not being part of Europe, and noting that two of the British had spent a significant part of their careers in the United States).

In 2009 the trustees took a decision to reform the IASB and increase its membership to 16. They will impose geographical constraints, with 4 members of the board coming from North America, 4 from Europe, 4 from Asia-Oceania, 1 from South America, and 3 from any part of the globe.

In fact, compared to how it looks now, the board will look quite different by the end of 2011. The maximum term of office for a board member is 5 years, renewable once. All the founding board members, including the chairman, will therefore have left by June 2011. The trustees are faced with 9 members whose terms expire between 2009 and 2011, of whom only 2 can be reappointed. In addition, they have to find 2 extra members to reach the target of 16. They will therefore adjust the structure gradually over a transitional period.

The question of geographical affiliation carries with it a few uncertainties. If a "good" board member should ideally have the experience of several countries, it follows that a clear national identity may be difficult. For example, former IASB member Tony Cope is British, even though most of his career was spent in the United States, including his time as a member of the FASB. Would he have been part of the European quota? Bob Herz is a U.S. citizen but was educated in the United Kingdom and trained as a chartered accountant before going back to the United States. Does Prabhakar Kalavacherla count as part of the Asia-Oceania quota or the North America quota?

The SAC was also part of the original structure set up in 2001, but it was revised in a constitutional review in 2005 and once more in 2009 as part of the second constitutional review. The SAC, as its name suggests, is an advisory group, comparable to the U.S. Financial Accounting Standards Advisory Council. It is supposed to advise the IASB on its work program. It meets three times a year, and its members are appointed by the trustees. In 2008, U.S. members included Frank Brod (Microsoft), Michael Paul Cangemi (FEI), Trevor Harris (Morgan Stanley), and Dane Mott (Bear Stearns). The SEC has observer status.

Its early meetings were quite lively. In 2001, when the IASB unveiled its plan to issue a standard on employee stock options to the SAC, the chief executive of FEI threatened dire consequences, and warnings of trouble ahead were given by a number of members.[2] However, over time the usefulness of the body has become questionable. Typically, the meeting consists of presentations of current projects by IASB members and staff, accompanied by oft-repeated complaints from some members who would probably prefer a different method of setting standards.

In the 2005 constitutional review, the SAC was given an independent part-time chairman, and its numbers were slightly reduced. The second review also looked at the composition of the SAC. Its purpose this time was to give particular institutions and associations a seat and leave it to the institution to provide a representative at each meeting. It also aimed to give more of an investor-user focus.

Clearly, the politics of standard setting demand that there be some kind of formal consultative group, but much of the real consultation takes place in less formal settings. The IASB appoints advisory groups to help it address particular issues, such as financial statement presentation or the financial crisis. Board members and senior staff also travel the world widely to meet with national standard-setters and other constituent groups where they discuss convergence issues in private. It remains to be seen if the SAC, in its next iteration under Canadian chairman Paul Cherry, can develop a meaningful place for itself.

The IFRIC is the part-time body that addresses technical issues regarding the use of IFRS. Chaired by IASB member Bob Garnett, its other members are auditors, preparers, and users who meet six times a year in London to consider issues raised by constituents. Current members include Peggy Smyth, a vice president of United Technologies Corp., and Scott Taub, formerly of the SEC. Phil Ameen of General Electric was a member until June 2008. Other organizations with members are Siemens (Germany) and Sumitomo Corporation (Japan), as well as the usual audit firms.

IFRIC's function is to interpret existing IFRS. An example of its work would be a query on the accounting for customer loyalty programs. Constituents queried whether the "bonus" element in a sale transaction that included a future bonus—such as the case with air miles related to an airline ticket—should be treated as a cost of the initial sale or whether the initial transaction should be accounted for as though it were two items. Both treatments are allowed under the relevant standard, IAS 18 *Revenue*, but give different accounting outcomes. In IFRIC 13 *Customer Loyalty*

*Programmes*, the IFRIC determined that the revenue should be split between the initial transaction and the "bonus," rather than recognizing the costs of the bonus as part of the initial transaction.

IFRIC Interpretations have to be approved by the IASB, but once approved have the full force of an accounting standard. Aside from the chairman, a number of the board members attend IFRIC meetings in an observer role.

## IASB Due Process

The IASB's due process is to be found in various documents. The basis of it is in the IASC Foundation Constitution (paragraph 31). This is elaborated a little in the *Preface to IFRS* (paragraph 18), a stand-alone document that is deemed to be read in conjunction with each individual IFRS. However, the detail is to be found in a document approved by the trustees in 2006: *Handbook of Consultative Arrangements*, also known as the *Due Process Handbook*.

Similar to that of the FASB, the key stages in due process are the following:

1. Decision to take the subject onto the agenda
2. Issue of a preliminary views discussion paper (DP)
3. Consideration of constituent comments
4. Issue of an exposure draft (ED)
5. Consideration of constituent comments
6. Issue of a final standard (IFRS)
7. Review of the operation of the standard after 2 years

The first issue is the *agenda decision*. In the United States this process has been simplified, and the chairman of the FASB has sole authority to determine what subjects are dealt with by the standard-setter. For the IASB the process is much more complicated. In the first instance, the staff has to prepare an agenda proposal. This has to define the following issues:

1. *Whether there is existing guidance.* The proposal needs to specify whether there is any guidance. If there is guidance, are there significant

national variants, and is there diversity in practice? Is there the possibility of increasing convergence internationally?

2. *The quality of the standard to be developed.* Are there other ways of
   improving financial reporting in this area? Is it likely that the IASB
   would be able to reach a majority decision on the subject? Will the
   benefits to users exceed the costs of implementation? Can a technically feasible solution be found in a reasonable amount of time?
3. *The resource constraints.* Has another standard-setter already done
   work in the area that can be used? How much additional research
   would be involved? Does the IASB have access to sufficient resources
   internally and externally to carry out the project?

The IASB decides on the basis of this whether there is a case for taking on a project. This is debated at a public standard-setting session. If
there is a positive decision, this must then be referred to the SAC, as well
as to national standard-setters, for their advice. The handbook does not
specify it, but agenda decisions are also referred to the trustees.

If all the bodies consulted are in agreement, the IASB then makes
a final decision. However, this can have nuances. The IASB has both a
"research agenda" and an "active agenda." A project can go through the
approval process and then be parked in the research agenda, eventually
for years, on the basis that there is not sufficient time or enthusiasm to
address it immediately.

An example of this is accounting for self-generated intangibles. At a joint
meeting between the FASB and IASB held in London in April 2004,[3] FASB
member Katherine Schipper argued strongly for these to be considered for
future action as a joint project. Eventually the IASB came to an arrangement
with the AASB that their staff should carry out research on this issue. In 2006,
the two boards agreed that an agenda decision on the project should be made
by the end of 2007. The AASB staff put forward an agenda proposal that the
IASB agreed to take forward to the SAC and trustees, who in turn approved
the proposal. When the IASB and FASB subsequently came to look at their
priorities for completion by 2011, the project was put back on the research
agenda where it will likely remain for another 5 years.[4]

The next stage of the process is a decision as to whether to issue
a DP. Under IASB due process, there is no requirement to do so.

However, as the IASB has evolved, it has found that much better feedback is obtained by issuing a DP, and there is greater constituent buy-in to the final standard than when the process goes directly to an ED. It is therefore established policy to do this for all major projects, even though issuing a DP will add 12 to 18 months to the timeline.

If the board thinks it will be useful, the handbook also provides for the appointment of an advisory group—or in IASB terminology, a "working group"—to act as a sounding board as the project develops. Here, too, IASB policy has evolved as the IASB has come to recognize that such dedicated working groups usually provide an efficient way of getting preliminary feedback on individual issues and getting input about industry practice. A working group is not typically asked to provide suggestions but rather to comment on the work of the staff as it proceeds.

The difficulty with working groups is that they are not always very useful, and a lot of time is taken up with organizing meetings and liaising with them. In the case of the IASB, there are also significant costs involved in bringing together people from all over the world. The IASB currently has working groups for insurance, private companies, financial instruments, pensions, financial statement presentation, and leasing. Sometimes a working group is a joint group with the FASB. This is usually the case where the subject is a joint project, such as financial statement presentation.

Under IASB standard procedures, staff prepare agenda papers ("memos" is the term the FASB uses) that are circulated to board members ahead of standard-setting meetings. The same papers (subject only to removal of any confidential matter—they are much more extensive than the notes provided to the public by the FASB) are made available on the IASB Web site for download. They are then debated at the IASB's monthly standard-setting meeting.[5] These meetings are open to the public, although capacity is limited and people have to register in advance.

The staff set out to prepare a DP by putting a series of papers before the IASB (or if it is a joint project with the FASB, then before both boards) that address the various issues. Staff discuss the issues informally with board members while they are working on them. Indeed, the custom is to assign two or three board members to each significant project to give the staff feedback between board meetings.

The DP should set out an analysis of the problem together with a discussion of the possible solutions. It is established preference at both the IASB and the FASB that the DP should include the "preliminary views" of each board. Members believe that asking constituents for comments on a range of possibilities does not give enough focus. Giving a preliminary view provides a clear steer as to what the final standard could look like, and constituents have more incentive to analyze how it might affect them.

After exploring the various issues with the board, the staff circulate a "preballot draft" of the DP. Board members are then asked to raise any objections to issues that are not in accordance with what they had agreed or issues they feel are badly expressed. Such issues ("sweep issues" in IASB terminology) are brought back to the board for redebate. Drafting issues are identified, but the official policy is that drafting points are dealt with by the staff off-line. The final draft DP is then submitted to a secret ballot of members.

The DP is then ready for publication. The IASB's preference is for a minimum exposure period of 120 days, or longer if the topic is particularly complicated. It should be noted that many of the IASB's constituents work in a language other than English. The DP is published only in English, and so extra time is needed for summaries to be prepared by constituent organizations in their national language.

If the topic is thought to be particularly difficult or sensitive, the IASB may also provide for some other forms of contact with constituents. The handbook talks about field visits, public meetings, and roundtables, but the preference is for roundtables. Sometimes roundtables are organized around submissions to a DP. People who have submitted comment letters are invited to the roundtable, and the discussion's theme includes particular issues that have been raised in the comment letters.

At each roundtable, the IASB will typically try to bring together people from different parts of the IFRS community: auditors, preparers, and users. Sometimes a roundtable is useful for people to clarify what is behind their argument and sometimes to try to get users, auditors, and preparers to talk to each other. Comment letters are normally posted to the IASB's Web site.

The next stage of due process is redeliberation and preparation of an ED. Staff will usually prepare an overview of the comment letters at the start of redeliberation and later bring a series of papers reviewing the issues. Sometimes the board will ask the staff to talk to constituents to get more feedback so that they may better understand a particular problem. It is during this phase that the key decisions are made. Once the exposure draft is agreed on, the board will only change its position if new arguments are brought forward. Arguments that it considered while moving from DP to ED will not generally be reconsidered while moving from ED to IFRS.

If the board has to move substantially away from the ED when it prepares the IFRS, it may have to reissue a revised exposure draft, or "reexpose" the draft. The board tries to avoid this, as it may add another year to the time to complete the standard. Consequently, when faced with a choice between a tough and a less tough stance at the ED stage, the board tends to take the tougher one. If it subsequently decides this was too tough, it can back down without reexposing. Done the other way, there is a high risk of needing to reexpose.

When the ED is issued, it goes through the same initial exposure process. Now, as long as the project has gone through the DP stage, the board is more interested in discovering whether there is some fatal flaw in the proposal than revisiting the arguments put forward on the DP. Of course, if the project has not passed through the DP stage, then the ED is the only phase where substantive arguments can be debated, so the board's approach is different.

Board members do not normally abstain from voting on an ED or final standard. They either approve it or indicate dissent. When a board member dissents, they are obliged to write an explanation of their dissent. This is also published with the ED or IFRS.

The staff again reviews the comments on the ED, and the whole is subject to redeliberation and, finally, a secret ballot. Both EDs and IFRS require a minimum of 9 votes in favor out of a total of 14. When the board reaches its total of 16, the minimum will be 10 votes in favor. An IFRS is usually issued with an application date 12 months ahead. The long period of delay is to give time for translations to be prepared, and for those jurisdictions that need to take the IFRS into national law to go through their statutory processes.

It is next to impossible to say how long it takes to move from an agenda proposal to a final standard because there are so many factors that can intervene. These will be discussed more in chapter 6, but events and political pressures can change priorities. The financial crisis has caused the IASB to speed up its work on consolidation and its review of financial instruments. This will affect other topics, such as pensions, which may have reform deferred for a while because of resource constraints. Assuming a project is relatively noncontroversial, 3 years would be about the minimum to write a new standard including a DP stage, but 4 to 5 years is the more likely span. Controversial standards can take much longer.

## Lobbying the IASB

The IASB aims to make its standard setting as transparent as possible, and for the moment it does not attempt to prevent interested parties talking to either board members or staff about current projects. However, given how many years the standard-setting process takes, companies or organizations wishing to influence a particular issue will need to devote several years to the effort. As indicated above, the crucial stage for influencing the board is as the project moves from DP to ED, and this may be 2 or 3 years before the standard is finalized. Many companies either do not realize this or do not think it is worth the resources to monitor what the IASB is doing. In many cases they are not aware that a change is planned until the final standard is published and their auditors start telling them that they have to implement it. It is far too late to do anything about the standard then.

Companies need then to nominate at least one person connected with group accounting policies to monitor what is going on. This can be done relatively cheaply by subscribing to dedicated newsletters from independent publishers, such as Business Expert Press, that provide commentary and evaluation or advisories from the Big Four audit firms, as well as downloading material directly from the IASB. The company will then be aware of what subjects the IASB is looking at. There will be plenty of notice that the standard-setter is taking a subject on to the agenda, but the lobbyist should be sure to look at the agenda proposal to see what the problem is as seen by the IASB.

If the problem is not relevant to your company, no great attention needs to be given to it; if it does affect the company, then an assessment of impact needs to be made. In the case where it could be very significant, the company could offer to supply a member of the working group, and therefore automatically have contact with the staff and board members who are dealing with the project.

Normally, however, the less costly course of action is to review the agenda for each monthly board meeting and download the papers that concern the particular project of concern. That way one can keep informed as to what is being prepared for the DP. Nonetheless, one should be aware that this could last for as long as 2 years, especially if it is a joint project with the FASB that has to be debated by both boards with agreement reached by both groups. However, at this very early stage, staff are looking for facts about the transactions concerned, and this is the moment to contact them and offer help by providing information about how business handles the transaction and the likely impact of changes.

Once the DP is published, this is the time to mobilize public comments and support for a particular solution. The company should itself write to the IASB, but it should also lobby its auditors, who will also be formulating a worldview through their IFRS desk. It may also be worth writing to national standard-setters and professional associations. If the company thinks the solutions proposed in the preliminary views would be disastrous, it should try to put together research evidence and suggest an alternative solution.

Saying that the company does not like a particular solution does not advance matters very much, because the IASB has to find a solution. The IASB reasons in terms of its conceptual framework. Accounting solutions must give financial reporting that is relevant and representationally faithful and helps investors to make useful decisions. The benefit to users must exceed the cost of providing the information. Lobbyists must, therefore, couch their arguments in these terms.

For example, if a company does not like a solution, it must analyze what the objection is. Is it because the company does not find the information presented in this way useful? In that case the company must point out that this is a cost with no benefit to the preparer and try to find evidence that helps the board assess usefulness of the information to the user. (The board does not like preparers taking a view on the benefit of the information to users; they argue that making the cost/benefit assessment is their prerogative.)

The IASB also thinks in terms of assets and liabilities. Has the transaction caused any change in the entity's assets and liabilities? If so, can this be measured reliably? During the internal debates before the *Revenue Recognition* DP was issued, staff argued that once an entity received a noncancelable contract, it should recognize an asset (the cash flows due under the contract) and a liability (the cost of performing its obligations under the contract). If this were done, there would most likely be a profit on signature of the contract because the costs should normally be less than the revenues.

This approach was not finally supported by the FASB and IASB, but the arguments were that (a) the case was untypical—in most cases the supply took place immediately, and where this was not the case, the contract was usually cancelable; and (b) there would only be a potential asset if the contract was noncancelable (the conceptual framework definition requires that the entity *controls* the future economic inflows). On the liability side, there was much argument as to how one would measure the fulfillment obligation. Should it include a return on the fulfillment process? How does one allocate the profit between the selling activity and the fulfilling activity?

The IASB also listens to arguments such as the risk of creating opportunities for manipulation or abuse ("structuring opportunities," as IASB member John Smith calls them). It also prefers consistency within a standard and between standards.

The central point is that a comment letter, to be effective, must provide an analysis that is couched in terms of the conceptual framework and the IASB's objectives of converged, high-quality standards. In addition, the comment letter should provide evidence, if possible.

Once the comment period is over, the public lobbying stops and the private effort may continue, if required. A company could contact the IASB staff and offer to explain or discuss its comment letter. It should monitor the papers published for the board meetings to see how the staff analyzed the comments and how the ED is evolving out of the DP. If the solution the board is heading for is not favored by the company, then it should do its best to talk with the IASB staff and suggest alternative solutions.

When the ED is published, the public comment process starts again. However, it is difficult to assess how cost effective lobbying is at this stage. As discussed above, there is little obvious reason for the board to revisit arguments they have already mulled over in moving from the DP. However, the ED does include a "Basis for Conclusions" that explains on what grounds various decisions were made. This may provide an additional opportunity to challenge an unwelcome change by querying the basis for the decision. As ever, comments need to be structured in relevant argument and ideally need to put forward an alternative solution (explaining why it is better) and evidence.

## Interpretations

IFRIC has a key role to play in helping to make sure that IFRS are interpreted and applied in the same way around the world. It liaises with stock exchange regulators such as the SEC and the IFRS desks of the international audit firms, as well as national standard-setters. Where there are issues concerning local application that relate to national laws or taxes, the IFRIC is inclined to leave the problem to the national authorities. However, where it considers an issue is of worldwide relevance, it will provide guidance.

IFRIC guidance comes in three forms:

1. A decision not to take an issue onto it agenda
2. An interpretation
3. A recommendation to the IASB to amend a standard

IFRIC would deny that its agenda decisions are part of the IFRS literature, and technically that is the case. However, when IFRIC refuses to address a topic, it usually provides an explanation for its decision. This explanation is often a clarification of how people should look at a particular standard, and, in that sense, it is application guidance. IFRIC's main output are interpretations, which are mandatory. However, it cannot change existing standards, and sometimes it will only suggest that the IASB amend the wording of the underlying standard to make the position more clear. The director of implementation activities not only looks after IFRIC but also deals with the Annual Improvement Process. This is an annual batch of minor amendments to existing standards.

IFRIC has its own *Due Process Handbook* similar to that of the IASB. This sets out how items are submitted, how issues are exposed, and how the IASB can be consulted. Anyone can submit an issue to the IFRIC, but it will issue guidance only on subjects that are of general applicability. Issues relating to individual entities are not addressed. IFRIC will look into an issue if there is diversity in practice or if there is doubt about the appropriate accounting to follow.

The IFRIC meets generally six times a year for 2 days. Its meetings are open to the public. IFRIC publishes *IFRIC Update* after every meeting. Its proceedings are also reported in independent publications such as *IFRIC Monitor* (http://www.ifrsmonitor.com). The staff prepare an analysis of items that have been submitted for consideration without disclosing the origin of the inquiry. The IFRIC then makes an agenda decision either to take up the subject or not. The decision requires only a simple majority. Members have to consider whether the problem can be resolved by an interpretation and whether this can be done in a timely manner. They must be persuaded that financial reporting will improve by addressing the issue. If it is an issue that is being addressed by the IASB, they may still choose to address it if more timely guidance is thought necessary.

The tentative agenda decision is published in *IFRIC Update* and reviewed 2 months later at the next IFRIC meeting. As discussed above, a negative agenda decision can in itself be a clarification, although it is not part of authoritative IFRS literature.

Once an item is on the agenda, the process is very similar to that of the IASB, although there is no DP stage.[6] The staff prepare papers that are debated by IFRIC members, and over a period a draft interpretation is developed. The IFRIC has 12 members (although this is due to increase slightly). A minimum of 9 must be present or participating by telephone to reach quorum. Only 3 people can dissent from a consensus. The draft interpretation must include (a) a description of the problem, (b) the consensus solution, (c) details of the IFRS relied upon, and (d) a basis for conclusions.

Once the draft has been agreed upon by IFRIC, it goes for negative clearance to the IASB. The draft is issued provided no more than

4 IASB members disagree with it. In practice, there is quite close liaison between the IFRIC and the IASB. The chairman of IFRIC is a member of the IASB, and several other board members attend meetings as observers. The director of implementation activities provides the IASB with an update on the work in progress at each of the IASB's public meetings.

A draft interpretation is exposed for at least 60 days. The comments are, as with the IASB, analyzed by the staff and are also published on the IFRIC Web site. The IFRIC then redeliberates the issues and tries to reach a final consensus. The final consensus is then submitted to the IASB for formal approval and is only issued once that has been obtained.

## Relationships With National Standard-Setters

The way in which the IASB interacts with other standard-setters has also evolved over time. In the original board, a number of members were specifically tasked with liaising with individual national bodies. For example, Jim Leisenring was official liaison to the FASB, while Geoff Whittington was the official liaison to the UK Accounting Standards Board. These formal relationships have been quietly dropped as they were perceived as having a negative impact on standard-setters that had no official liaison person, although Jim Leisenring continues to travel back and forth across the Atlantic and has a desk at the FASB as well as the IASB.

The IASB also used to hold meetings in other countries to liaise with the national standard-setters. In the early years, the IASB held meetings in Canada, Japan, Hong Kong, Norway, Italy, France, and Germany. However, it found that these meetings were logistically very challenging, and the meetings were not necessarily attended by any people other than those regularly observing in London. Furthermore, the formal liaison sessions, where the full board met with the full national board, were not very productive. On the other hand, a meeting with world standard-setters organized in the margins of the 2002 World Accountants Congress in Hong Kong was very successful.

Liaison with national standard-setters is very important to the IASB. As David Tweedie remarked in the 2007 annual report, the board has had to develop new ways of communicating with interested parties. Every year, it has repeated the annual meeting pioneered in Hong Kong, where "particular issues are discussed and the problems standard-setters are having in adopting international standards are communicated to the Board." In addition individual board members visit regions to discuss issues with national standard-setters. "A large number of countries in six continents are visited every year."

The IASB chairman also reported that the board had continued to provide a series of road shows "to explain the Board's work program, to hear views of preparers and users and to encourage them to participate in our processes." The IASB also participates in conferences and, through the IASC Foundation, directly promotes some of them.

Nonetheless, the IASB has a special relationship with two organizations: the FASB and the European Financial Reporting Advisory Group (EFRAG). The relationship with the FASB has been dealt with throughout this book. Having its standard accepted as equivalent of FASB standards has been an IASB target for many years and the convergence program has, since 2002, made the relationship concrete with a number of joint standards.

EFRAG is not a national or regional standard-setter as such, but is a curious organization that provides technical input to the IASB and to the European Commission. The European Commission has only a very small staff devoted to financial reporting and relies on resources provided by Europe-wide associations connected with financial reporting to make inputs to the IASB due process.[7] EFRAG's Technical Expert Group reviews all IASB publications and collates responses from national standard-setters and other interested parties. IASB staff and board members maintain close liaison with EFRAG on a day-to-day basis, and EFRAG has a formal public meeting with IASB members three times a year to discuss issues. In 2009 the European Commission announced funding for EFRAG, and the organization is now due to be restructured.

Finally there is another organization, called the "national standard-setters," that groups together standard-setters from several countries. This organization is chaired by Ian Mackintosh, chairman of the UK Accounting Standards Board, and meets twice a year to discuss matters related to IFRS. The body is independent of the IASB, but "has David Tweedie's Blessing," according to Mr. Mackintosh. At a briefing in London in 2008, Mr. Mackintosh explained the group had no constitution, nor any rules, but consisted of about 20 national standard-setters that had the capacity to carry out research into policy issues. EFRAG, the IASB, and the International Public Sector Accounting Standards Board were members, and China was coming to the next meeting.

The group has a mandate from the IASB to comment on the IASB's agenda; it is difficult to get a consensus, and so views are often watered down. They also have a mandate to do long-term research and had been asked by the IASB to look at taxation, intangibles, and short-term convergence projects—subjects that would come up after 2011. The UK and German standard-setters were working on taxation. France was reviewing share-based payment. Australia had done a lot of work on intangibles, but this had been shelved by the IASB. They were currently doing a paper on accounting by superannuation funds. Canada was not happy with IAS 26; nobody uses it much. There were eight or nine core members with the capacity to do serious research.

## National Standard-Setters in an IFRS Environment

It might be thought that once a country adopts IFRS, there is no longer any role for the national standard-setter. Practice so far would show that this is not the case. No national standard-setters have disappeared in countries adopting IFRS, although a number of them have been reorganized. Their main tasks are to provide standards for private business and liaise between their constituents and the IASB.

In the United States, many private companies follow U.S. GAAP for contractual or other reasons, even though the SEC's mandate extends only to SEC registrants. The FASB has, of course, set up its Private Company Financial Reporting Committee, but there is no federally mandated accounting for private business. The situation in Europe is quite different. Virtually all limited liability companies are subject to financial reporting regulation by government, and, in some countries, even unincorporated businesses are also regulated in this way.

This means that even if the financial reporting of listed companies has been taken away from the national standard-setter, there is still a very large number of private companies for which accounting standards are required. This is one reason the IASB has developed an IFRS for private companies. In theory, national standard-setters could indeed adopt this and have no separate, local accounting standards, but this is unlikely to happen. Currently, most European countries allow private companies a choice as to whether they use full IFRS. This is to help those that are subsidiaries of listed companies and those potentially looking to list in the future. It remains to be seen how the private company sector will evolve.

At the moment, the UK standard-setter believes that the IFRS for Small and Medium-Sized Entities (SMEs) is still too complicated to be mandated for the smallest "Mom and Pop" businesses that are likely to be incorporated, and it is still debating whether to maintain a cut-down form of UK GAAP. Unofficially, the French also believe that the IFRS for private business does not simplify enough, and therefore the national standard-setter will continue to provide standards for private business, albeit standards influenced by IFRS.

The other role for the national standard-setters is as liaison with the IASB to provide adaptation of IFRS in a local environment. The AASB provides an example of this function. They initially decided to adopt IFRS as issued by the IASB but chose to modify them by not allowing all of the options that were available in some standards, and also by providing detail that related to local law and taxation. They issue Australian standards that are numbered with reference to the original IFRS but with these modifications. Subsequently they decided to remove the Australian restrictions on the use of options and to confine their role to responding to the IASB's due process and acting as a conduit for issues to be referred to IFRIC. Where IFRIC declines to take up an issue, the AASB will provide its own local interpretation.

Australia also provides inputs to the IASB's work program. Its staff developed the agenda proposal for self-generated intangibles and has also contributed to the DP on mineral resources.

It is too early to say what role the FASB would play after 2014, should the SEC take up IFRS. However, it is likely to remain a strong player in the development of future converged standards. It has considerable technical and financial resources that would presumably continue to be directed, at least in part, toward developing IFRS.

# Conclusion

This chapter has set out the organizational structure that surrounds the IASB and explained the standard-setter's due process. It has noted that companies and organizations wishing to influence the development of a particular standard need to do so during the development of the DP and the debate following its publication. Generally speaking, the later a constituent intervenes in the process, the less likely it is that they will have any impact at all.

This chapter has also reviewed IFRIC's due process and noted the close liaison between IFRIC and the IASB. It has analyzed the various relationships the IASB has with national standard-setters and the roles that some standard-setters have developed in relation to the IASB.

# CHAPTER 6

# The Origins of the IASB

The IASB, as we know it today, started with a telephone call at a hotel in Sydney, Australia, in November 1972. That telephone call triggered the rapid formation of the IASC, which metamorphosed into the IASB nearly 30 years later.

This chapter will provide some background to the IASB, starting with the formation of the IASC and its early years, then its transformation into a body focused on the capital markets, then the tough decade of the 1990s, and, last, the first decade of the IASB.

## Creating the IASC

The IASB story goes back to a world conference of accountants held in Sydney in 1972. Douglas Morpeth, a partner in Touche Ross, was head of the delegation of the Institute of Chartered Accountants of England and Wales (ICAEW), where he was the current president. Also at the conference was another senior British accountant, Henry Benson, a senior figure in Coopers & Lybrand (now integrated into PricewaterhouseCoopers), a past president of the ICAEW and a member of the committee organizing the conference.

Benson was a dominating figure in international accounting. He had spent his whole adult life in the accounting firm (aside from military service in World War II) and had been a partner since 1934. He was, in fact, a grandson of one of the four Cooper brothers who started the eponymous firm in the 19th century. He had been a key figure in the firm's international expansion after 1945 and particularly its merger in 1957 with the U.S. firm Lybrand, Ross Bros., and Montgomery. In 1945, the firm had 8 offices worldwide and 239 staff. When Benson retired in 1975, it had 332 offices and more than 18,000 staff.[1]

Morpeth was younger but was already a senior member of the accounting establishment in the United Kingdom. Aside from being president of the ICAEW, he was also deputy chairman of the United Kingdom's newly formed standard-setter, the Accounting Standards Committee. During the conference, Benson gave a report on his committee's activities and the future worldwide organization of the profession (5 years later the organization became the International Federation of Accountants [IFAC]). Morpeth subsequently called Benson in his hotel room to discuss the speech and said he was surprised the committee had not thought of creating an international accounting standard-setter.[2] The rest is history.

Benson and Morpeth convened an impromptu meeting with the leaders of the U.S. and Canadian delegations. The U.S. delegation was under Wally Olson, the president of the AICPA. Among them they hammered out the outline of what became the IASC. It was to have 9 members, which would be national professional bodies (United States, Canada, Australia, the United Kingdom and Ireland, France, Germany, the Netherlands, Mexico, and Japan).

Morpeth and Benson went back to London, where they obtained formal support from the ICAEW and drafted the constitution. They eventually agreed that Benson would be the chairman, given his impending retirement from Coopers & Lybrand, and the board of the IASC held its first meeting in June 1973 in London. In fact, London was to become its permanent base. Olson was keen for the IASC secretariat to be in New York, but the ICAEW offered to fund offices in London, which proved a decisive argument.

The creation of the IASC came at a time when there was much activity in the standard-setting area. In English-speaking, developed countries, technical guidance typically came from the professional accounting bodies using structures that were either implicitly accepted by the courts or integrated in some way into the legal structure. The UK professional bodies had just formed a national committee. In the United States, the Wheat Committee had in 1972 recommended the creation of a freestanding standard-setter, which resulted in the foundation of the FASB, in 1973.

The evolution at the national level also had parallels at the international level. The EU had been working since the late 1960s on harmonizing financial reporting in Europe, and in the 1970s both the United Nations (UN) and the Organization for Economic Cooperation and Development (OECD) made initiatives in this area.

The early work of the IASC was relatively uncontroversial.[3] The board produced material that could be described as codifying best practice among developed nations. Its standards often included several different ways of accounting for a transaction where there was fundamental disagreement between national delegations. Henry Benson stepped down as chairman in 1976, his place taken by Joseph Cummings, a partner in Peat, Marwick, Mitchell, & Co. in New York.

The professional member associations were supposed to use their best endeavors to have the IASC's standards adopted in their national jurisdiction, but as Benson complained at a conference in 1980, this just did not happen. In fact, at that time the international standards were mostly being used to complement national standards and also to guide the evolution of national standards.

This was particularly the case in some developing countries that were members of the British Commonwealth and had inherited their financial reporting from the British colonial period. Countries such as Malaysia and Singapore found it convenient, when developing national standards, to use IAS as a model. Sometimes the standards were used voluntarily by international companies from countries such as Switzerland, France, and Italy where rules for group financial reporting to the international markets had not yet been developed.

The IASC was making steady but unspectacular progress. In particular, it had achieved a major diplomatic success under the chairmanship of Hans Burggraaf (1980–1982), a senior Dutch accountant. Over a period of time, the IASC officials succeeded in persuading both the OECD and the UN that it would be counterproductive for these international bodies to issue accounting standards. Although the UN has remained active in accounting—its Expert Group on International Standards of Accounting and Reporting continues to do research and issue studies in this general area—it now works within IAS and IFRS.

## Focus on International Markets

However, a major change was coming. In 1987 the IASC started to work with the IOSCO for the purpose of having its standards adopted for secondary listings worldwide. In 1985 the IASC had appointed a new secretary: David Cairns, an auditor and academic specializing in international accounting. The secretary (later secretary-general) was the senior full-time executive running the IASC in conjunction with a rotating part-time chairman from one of the member organizations.

Cairns set out to sharpen the work of the IASC and develop its international role. As Camfferman and Zeff relate this, Cairns read an article in the *Financial Times* about another IASC, the International Association of Securities Commissions (an inexact translation of IOSCO's Spanish title) that was holding a conference in Paris.[4] This led to a meeting with the SEC in March 1987 where it was decided that if the IASC would tighten up its standards—either by removing options or at least specifying a benchmark option—these could be used by IOSCO. The international securities regulators' body was invited to join the IASC's Consultative Group.

There followed a period of considerable work for the IASC. It set out to improve its standards, in particular by removing as many options as possible. At the same time, Cairns and the then chairman, Georges Barthès de Ruyter, attempted to change the IASC's structure. Barthès was successful in persuading the European Commission and the SEC to accept observer roles. Where the national delegations had previously been from professional accounting bodies, these were no longer necessarily the national standard-setters. In particular, the AICPA was the U.S. member association, and Cairns and Barthès encouraged the FASB to get involved as well.

## The Difficult 1990s

If the late 1980s signaled the point where the IASC's trajectory shifted toward what it would become in 2000, there was, nonetheless, a lot of choppy water to get through in the 1990s. On the IASC's technical agenda was accounting for financial instruments. This would eventually result in a measurement standard, IAS 39, that was not agreed on until the very end of 1998, and then only after a lot of controversy. It has remained the most controversial standard ever since. It attracted negative comment during the early part of the credit crisis, and the IASB has undertaken to replace it with a simpler standard as soon as possible.

Relationships with IOSCO did not run smoothly either. The IASC had set a target of completing its "improvements" program by the end of 1993. However, in 1994 it received a slap in the face from IOSCO, with a refusal to endorse the standards in total. There was a good deal of disappointment after the years of hard work and difficult debates generated by the focus on IOSCO's needs. David Cairns resigned and the IASC had to rethink its position.

A new secretary-general, Bryan Carsberg, and new chairman, Michael Sharpe, took the helm at the organization. Carsberg had been a practitioner, academic, standard-setter, and, eventually, government regulator in turn. He had also spent a time on secondment to the FASB. Michael Sharpe was a South African practitioner who, as a young accountant, had served under Henry Benson at Coopers & Lybrand. These two started a new initiative with IOSCO. IOSCO provided a list of "core standards" that constituted the minimum required in their view, and the IASC agreed to provide these by 1999 (later advanced to 1998).

As in the earlier IOSCO program, the IASC's workload accelerated again, with initiatives begun on both the technical and organizational fronts. During this period it issued key standards on provisions, impairment, intangible assets, investment property, and—eventually—recognition and measurement of financial instruments (IAS 39).

None of these was easy, but IAS 39 was particularly difficult, as also was SFAS 133 in the United States. The standard was finally pushed through at the very end of 1998 with the understanding that it would be a "temporary" standard to meet the IOSCO deadline, leaving time thereafter for a better replacement to be constructed. When the IASB first met in 2001, one of their first decisions was to formally adopt all the IAS. However, one board member suggested that they should not adopt IAS 39 on the grounds of it being temporary.

In fact a working party (known as the Joint Working Group) had been set up by the IASC and suggested a replacement standard that was based on full fair value for financial instruments. However, the IASB realized that it was too early to try to move away from IAS 39.

In 1999 the completed core standards were handed to IOSCO with the hope that the body would hand down a decision after its May 2000 annual meeting. While IOSCO was looking at the standards, the IASC was also getting ready to completely change its structure. The old body, dominated and funded by national professional associations and the selling of publications, was to disappear. It was to be replaced by a small, mostly full-time, professional board modeled on the FASB and funded by voluntary contributions.

The debates and negotiations to reach that position were at least as tortuous as those for IAS 39. Part of IAS's political appeal was that (a) they had no single national origin and (b) many countries felt they had an input into their creation so they were not being obliged to take a solution in which they had no involvement. Many people, therefore, wanted the standard-setter to remain a geographically representative body to preserve the sense of communication up and down the system.

Other people, notably the SEC and FASB, thought that this was unworkable. In its later days, when the IASC met, there could be as many as 100 participants, including national representatives, observers, and their surrounding technical advice teams. It took a long time to reach agreement, and there was plenty of evidence of people arguing in an attempt to preserve their local standards irrespective of their merits from the perspective of the investor in international capital markets. This group wanted a small committee of people with experience of setting standards for the capital markets.

The debate lasted a long time and went through a series of alternatives that tried to square the circle by having a small "technical" committee and a larger geographical endorsement process. Eventually the SEC view prevailed, but only very narrowly. The IASB was to be a small group of professionals (yet twice the size of the FASB). As we have seen, the argument has continued ever since and is still causing the structure to change.

# The New Dawn

If the 1990s had seemed a tough decade for everyone involved with the evolution of international standards, it was to lead to an astonishing start to the next century. In just a few months in 2000, the politics of international standards were to change radically.

In May 2000, IOSCO was meeting in Sydney, Australia. The member organizations had received the core standards and a report by IOSCO's working party. The securities regulators voted to endorse the IASC standards. This was a very significant advance for the IASC, but it was not as great as it might have been. IOSCO still allowed individual countries to ask for additional information or even reconciliations to national GAAP. Many people were disappointed as they had hoped for more, but the IASC treated this as a major achievement.

However, the IOSCO endorsement was to be completely eclipsed in June by an announcement from the European Commission that it had decided to put in hand legislation that would require all companies listed on European exchanges to use IFRS as of 2005.

This was a surprise on a number of counts. On the one hand, the commission had announced in 1995 that it was abandoning its attempt at regional harmonization and recommending that member states, if they wished to modernize their rules, should be guided by IAS. On the other hand, the commission had always been lukewarm about IAS. It had only reluctantly become an observer relatively late in the life of the IASC, and it had not actively participated in drawing up standards. The commission had also been one of the supporters of a geographically based standard-setter.

The fact that the commission was to oblige European companies to use IAS was a major boost to the standard-setter, which could thereafter point to the world's second largest economic block as a constituent. The IASC immediately gained far more significance than IOSCO's endorsement had provided.

The third major event took place in Edinburgh in July 2000. This was the formal abandonment of the old IASC by its owners—the national accountancy bodies—and approval of the new professional structure. By this time all associations that were members of the IFAC were automatically members of the IASC. IFAC convened a meeting that included a vote to move to the new structure. The new global standard-setter had been born.

## IASB: The First Decade

The first public meeting of the IASB took place in April 2001 at a hotel in London. It attracted a large number of observers over its 3 days as "the great and the good" of international accounting came to witness this historic moment. A good deal of time was devoted to a discussion of the projects to be put on the board's agenda. Staff who had carried over from the IASC gave presentations on work in progress, and board members debated suggestions from various bodies as to what their priorities should be.

Chairman David Tweedie suggested that they should take on share-based payment (accounting for stock options) as a priority. Board member Geoff Whittington commented that it was not technically a major problem; it was more a political problem, and the IASB was best placed to take the lead. Former FASB member Jim Leisenring warned that the IASB would be finished as a standard-setter if it took a position on this and then later backed down.

In the same session the chairman also identified intangible assets as a leadership project—but it has been nearly 10 years and still this has not made it to the IASB's active agenda. Many board members expressed dissatisfaction about the existing IAS, particularly IAS 39. The chairman insisted that they could not abandon any of the existing IAS, but they agreed that they would carry out an urgent "improvements" project. The object of this was to address issues of inconsistency, additional disclosures, elimination of remaining options, and requests for further guidance that had been brought forward by constituents.

The chairman announced that the trustees had decided that the IASB's new standards should be called International Financial Reporting Standards (IFRS) but the existing IAS should retain their name. The meeting agreed that "IFRS" would also be the generic title for all the IASB authoritative literature, including Interpretations.

Convergence was discussed, with segment reporting and business combinations identified as two areas where the inherited literature differed noticeably from U.S. GAAP. SFAS 141 and SFAS 142, which radically changed the U.S. treatment of business combinations and goodwill, were issued in June 2001. While the IASC had participated in the work on segment reporting that had been done by the United States and Canada, it had not felt able to join them in moving to the "through the eyes of management" approach mandated by SFAS 131 in 1997.

Curiously enough, the issue of whether there should be an IFRS for smaller entities was also discussed at this first meeting, foreshadowing the strong opposition from a minority of members to this project that had been started by the IASC. In that debate, current FASB chairman Bob Herz—still a member of the IASB at that time—said, while acknowledging that the standards were inappropriate for small business, "We cannot ourselves be seen to endorse a second system."[5] Tony Cope, another former member of the FASB, thought the IASB would be doing itself a disservice to come up with a junior system. He said there was a clear mandate in the constitution to address the needs of the international capital markets, and it should concern itself exclusively with that.

Another surprising omission from this agenda discussion was that of the debate about the consequences of the European Commission's decision to adopt IFRS. It could be argued that the desire to give priority to an improvements program was a manifestation of the desire to get the standards ready for the 2005 adoption. However, my notes suggest this was presented only to get the standards in order and improve internal consistency, rather than as a focus on the EU needs.

The board continued to discuss the agenda at subsequent meetings and also brought it to the first meeting of the Standards Advisory Council. Table 6.1 shows what items were agreed on in 2001 and what had happened to them by the end of 2008.

It can be seen that fairly rapid progress was made on some of the key standards, in particular first-time adoption, share-based payment, and business combinations as well as the improvements to IAS. But progress was much slower on insurance contracts and private entities, while hardly any progress was made on replacing the "temporary" IAS 39.

Table 6.2 shows what subjects were not on the initial agenda but had to be dealt with as a result of external circumstances. This table shows that agenda time was filled with issues that came to light as companies

*Table 6.1. Progress on the Initial Agenda*

| Items identified July 2001 | |
|---|---|
| Improvements—general | Final standards (2003) |
| Improvements—financial instruments | Final standard (2003) |
| Reporting financial performance | Phase A final standard issued 2007 |
| | Phase B DP issued 2008 |
| Present value | Disappeared |
| Liabilities/equity | Work being carried out by FASB, DP issued in 2008 |
| Consolidation | ED issued 2008 |
| Segment reporting | IFRS 8 (2007) |
| Impairment | Deferred |
| Business combinations 1 | IFRS 3 (2004) |
| Business combinations 2 | ED issued 2003, IFRS issued 2008 |
| Derecognition | Work started 2008 |
| Joint ventures | ED (2007) |
| Share-based payments | IFRS 2 (2004) |
| Intangible assets | Research agenda |
| Leases | Work started in 2007 |
| SME accounting | IFRS expected 2009 |
| Insurance contracts | Project split into two, IFRS 4 issued as holding standard (2004). DP issued 2007 on phase 2 |
| Financial institutions | IFRS 7 (2005) |
| First-time adoption | IFRS 1 (2003, amended 2005) |
| Conceptual framework | ED on objectives and qualitative characteristics (2008) |

DP = discussion paper; ED = exposure draft.
Source: Adapted from Dick and Walton (2007), pp. 8–17.

started to apply IFRS in many different countries and to very different situations. The IASB spent a great deal of time tinkering with IAS 39.

In reviewing this first part of the life of the IASB, it can be seen that convergence with U.S. GAAP has been a major preoccupation. This was made concrete through the Norwalk Agreement in 2002, and milestones were established through the Memorandum of Understanding, which gave targets for 2008 and now 2011. At the same time, the early period from 2001 to 2004 was also dominated by the need for a workable set of

*Table 6.2. Items Addressed but not on the 2001 Agenda*

| Items not identified July 2001 | |
|---|---|
| Assets held for disposal | IFRS 5 (2004) |
| Extractive industries | IFRS 6 (2004, amended 2005) |
| Fair value hedge accounting | IAS 39 amendment (2004) |
| Transition and initial recognition of financial assets and liabilities | IAS 39 amendment (2004) |
| Cash flow hedge accounting of forecast intragroup transactions | IAS 39 amendment (2005) |
| Fair value option | IAS 39 amendment (2005) |
| Capital disclosures | IAS 1 amendment (2005) |
| Financial guarantee contracts | IAS 39, IFRS 4 amendments (2005) |
| Net investment in a foreign operations | IAS 21 amendment (2005) |
| Fair value measurement guidance | DP (2006) ED expected 2009 |
| Borrowing costs | IAS 23 amended (2007) |
| Disclosures by state-controlled entities | IAS 24 amendment ED (2007) |
| Puttable financial instruments | IAS 32 amendment (2008) |
| Reducing complexity in accounting for financial instruments | DP 2008 |
| Removal of pension cost deferral | IAS 19 amendment DP 2008 |
| Canadian transition issues | IFRS 1 amendment ED 2008 |
| Financial crisis disclosures | IFRS 7 amendment ED 2008 |
| Reclassification of financial instruments | IAS 39 amended (2008) |

DP: Discussion Paper; ED: Exposure Draft
Source: Adapted from Dick and Walton (2007), pp. 8–17.

standards for 2005 adopters. It was also, in practice, much affected by the improvements program.

IAS 39 proved to be the most troublesome inheritance, and working to improve it opened the door to many constituents attempting to amend it to suit their own purposes. The IASB came up with the fair value option during this process, which the FASB took up. IAS 39 also caused some European companies, notably French banks, to explore different ways of putting pressure on the international standard-setter.

Once the 2004–2005 deadline for the first wave of adopters was over, the standard-setter should have had time to address the more innovative items, such as revenue recognition and financial statement presentation. However, much of the agenda's time was taken up to resolve application problems that arose as thousands of companies in Europe, Australia, New Zealand, and South Africa started to come to grips with using IFRS.

One might consider that 2005 to 2008 was a period where more work was done on convergence, including bringing SFAS 131 on segment reporting into the IFRS literature (IFRS 8) and updating the joint FASB-IASB conceptual framework. However, it was also a period much affected by the need to "fix" problems in the existing literature.

The next phase for the Memorandum of Understanding with the FASB runs to the end of 2010 and here the focus is on preparing for the second wave of IFRS adopters (China, Japan, Canada, Brazil, South Korea, India, etc.). However, events have once again intervened, and much time has been taken up with the fallout from the credit crisis.

The write-off of "toxic assets"—caused by the requirement to value them at fair value on a continuing basis—shone a spotlight on fair value accounting. This impacted both the FASB and IASB, as bank regulators in particular were using investor accounts for the purposes of prudential ratios. This meant that as the fair value write-offs reduced banks' capital, the regulators required the banks to recapitalize and sell off assets.

The crisis also threw a spotlight on the use of OBS vehicles and the adequacy of risk disclosures. This in turn has generated a flurry of activity for both U.S. and international standard-setters to address these problems. On the positive side there is now more political acceptance to replace IAS 39 with a completely new standard. The FASB and IASB have thus a clear demonstration of the need to work very closely together and converge in these sensitive areas.

## The Near Future

It is impossible to predict what impact the credit crisis will have on IASB-FASB convergence, or on market regulation in the United States in general. Nor is it possible to assess what impact the Obama administration will have on the policies of the SEC (or an eventual successor organization). For more than 20 years, the SEC has followed a policy of internationalization, and since the creation of the IASB the U.S. market regulator has grown more and more enthusiastic. There is no guarantee that that collective enthusiasm will survive. However, in the Obama administration's blueprint for reforming regulation of the financial sector, which was published in a treasury report in June 2009, the new government reiterated support for rapid global convergence on a single standard.

If one leaves aside these fairly significant unknowns, then one can see that the 2008–2010 phase should see the completion of work on revenue recognition, financial statement presentation, liabilities, and possibly even financial instruments and leasing, but probably not insurance in time for the second wave.

The next key year should be 2011, as the new adopters start working seriously with IFRS. A host of new problems will most likely arise as the standards are used by people with quite different accounting cultures than those in which IAS were framed. It is also the year when the United States is supposed to make its decision, and the year when the current chairman and all the IASB founder members will have left the board.

If the United States decides to adopt IFRS, then no doubt there will be a new phase of completing key projects before most U.S. companies start to use the standards. One could expect to see a new pensions standard, as well as financial instruments, leasing, and insurance contracts—if these projects did not meet their 2010 deadlines. A standard on mineral extraction should also be well advanced, and maybe more work will be done on intangibles.

# Notes

## Chapter 1

1. SEC (2003).
2. *World Accounting Report* (2002, March), p. 8.
3. Aisbitt and Walton (2005).
4. ICAEW (2007), pp. 29–30.
5. A useful analysis of the value relevance literature concerning IFRS can be found in Soderstrom and Sun (2007).
6. ICAEW (2007), p. 57.
7. "Seeing Down the Road: IFRS and the U.S. Capital Markets," presented by John W. White on March 23, 2007, to a breakfast roundtable organized jointly by the New York Stock Exchange and the Brooklyn Law School.
8. A discussion of how KPMG has structured itself can be found in Tokar (2005).

## Chapter 2

1. "Regulation of the International Securities Markets." Securities Act Release No. 33-6807, November 14, 1988.
2. Concept Release 33-8831 (2007, August 7).
3. Concept Release 33-8831 (2007, August 7), p. 18.
4. Ball (2006), p. 8.
5. Damant (2006), pp. 29–30.
6. Damant (2006), p. 11.
7. AICPA. (2008, September). AICPA supports SEC proposed roadmap for transitioning to IFRS for public companies. *The CPA Letter*, p. 4.
8. "FASB Chairman Advocates 'Improving and Adopting' IFRS for US Companies." (2008, September). *Financial Executive*, pp. 13–15.
9. Camfferman and Zeff (2007), pp. 439–440.
10. Camfferman and Zeff (2007), p. 440.
11. Cammferman and Zeff (2007), p. 440.
12. See SEC, "Pursuant to Section 509(5) of the National Securities Markets Improvement Act of 1996 Report on Promoting Global Pre-eminence of American Securities Markets" (2007, October).
13. Camfferman and Zeff (2007), p. 479.

14. Remarks before the 2008 AICPA National Conference on Current SEC and PCAOB Developments, December 8, 2008.

15. In February 2009, the comment deadline was extended to April 20, 2009.

16. SEC (2008) Release No. 33-8982, p. 35.

17. SEC (2008) Release No. 33-8982, p. 55.

18. SEC (2008) Release No. 33-8982, p. 73.

19. SEC (2008) Release No. 33-8982, p. 29.

20. "New Chairman appointed." (2009, February). *World Accounting Report*, p. 7.

21. Comment letter to SEC, March 6, 2009.

22. Comment letter to SEC, February 20, 2009.

23. Comment letter to SEC, February 19, 2009.

24. Comment letter to SEC, February 17, 2009.

25. Comment letter from Elyse Douglas to SEC, February 3, 2009.

26. Aisbitt (2006).

27. Cited in "Profession Reacts to IFRS Plan." (2008, October). *Journal of Accountancy*, p. 21.

28. SEC (2007), p. 29.

29. ICAEW (2007).

30. Cited in "Profession Reacts to IFRS Plan." (2008, October). *Journal of Accountancy*, pp. 20–22.

# Chapter 3

1. *World Accounting Report* (2003, November), p. 8.

2. Cherry (2008).

3. Cherry (2008).

4. Reprinted with permission, from *The CICA's Guide to IFRS in Canada* (n.d.), p. 1. Any changes to the original material are the sole responsibility of the author and have not been reviewed or endorsed by the Canadian Institute of Chartered Accountants (CICA), Toronto, Canada.

5. *International Standard-Setting Report* (2008, March), p. 18.

6. Available online at http://www.acsbcanada.org/index.cfm/ci_id/193/la_id/1.htm.

7. Greiss and Sharp (n.d.), p. 9.

8. Greiss and Sharp (n.d.), pp. 11–12.

9. Greiss and Sharp (n.d.), p. 9.

10. Adapted with permission from *20 Questions Directors and Audit Committees Should Ask About IFRS Conversions* by Rafik Greiss and Simon Sharp, p. 9–12. Any changes to the original material are the sole responsibility of the author and have not been reviewed or endorsed by CICA.

11. See CSA Staff Notice 52-321, *Early Adoption of International Financial Reporting Standards, Use of US GAAP and Reference to IFRS-IASB.*

# Chapter 4

1. KPMG (2008).
2. PricewaterhouseCoopers (2007).
3. IAS 38.78.
4. Morais (2008), pp. 127–139.
5. SEC (2005).

# Chapter 5

1. IASC Foundation Constitution, para. 20.
2. Walton (2001).
3. *International Standard-Setting Report* (2004, Q4), p. 29.
4. The AASB issued its own discussion paper on intangible assets in October 2008. The paper recommended accounting for all intangibles at fair value. It can be downloaded at http://www.aasb.com.au.
5. These debates are fully reported in *IFRS Monitor,* published monthly by BEP, and are available online at http://www.businessexpertpress.com/ifrs.
6. A detailed account of how an Interpretation is developed can be found in Bradbury (2007). Professor Bradbury was a member of IFRIC until June 2008.
7. For a detailed review of European accounting harmonization and Institutions, see Walton (2003).

# Chapter 6

1. Walton (2002).
2. Bocqueraz and Walton (2006).
3. Anyone wishing to go more deeply into the history of the IASC should consult the excellent in-depth study by Camfferman and Zeff (2007).
4. Camfferman and Zeff (2007), pp. 293–347.
5. Walton (2001), p. 12.

# References

Aisbitt, S. (2006). Assessing the effect of the transition to IFRS on equity: The case of the FTSE 100. *Accounting in Europe, 3*, 117–133.

Aisbitt, S., & Walton, P. (2005). Preparing for IFRS in the UK: Disclosures by FTSE 100 Companies. Milton Keynes, UK: Accounting and Finance Research Unit, Open University.

Ball, R. (2006). International Financial Reporting Standards: Pros and Cons for Investors. *Accounting and Business Research.* International Accounting Policy Forum 2006 pp. 5–29.

Bocqueraz, C., & Walton, P. (2006). Creating a supranational institution: The role of the individual and the mood of the times. *Accounting History, 11*(3), 271–288.

Bradbury, M. (2007). An anatomy of an IFRIC interpretation. *Accounting in Europe, 4*(2), 109–122.

Camfferman, K., & Zeff, S. (2007). *Financial reporting and global capital markets: A history of the international accounting standards committee 1973–2000.* Oxford, UK: Oxford University Press.

Canadian Institute of Chartered Accountants (CICA). (n.d.). *The CICA's guide to IFRS in Canada.* Toronto, Canada: Author.

Cherry, P. (2008, January 30). Time for common accounting standards. *National Post.*

Damant, D. (2006). Discussion of IFRS: Pros and cons for investors. *Accounting and Business Research.* International Accounting Policy Forum 2006.

Dick, W., & Walton, P. (2007). The agenda of the IASB: A moving target. *Australian Accounting Review, 17*(42), 8–17.

Greiss, R., & Sharp, S. (n.d.). *20 questions directors and audit committees should ask about IFRS conversions.* Toronto, Canada: CICA.

Institute of Chartered Accountants in England and Wales (ICAEW). (2007). *Implementation of IFRS and the fair value directive.* London: Author.

KPMG. (2008). *IFRS compared to U.S. GAAP.* London: KPMG IFRG.

Morais, A. I. (2008). Actuarial gains and losses: The choice of the accounting method. *Accounting in Europe, 5*(2), 127–139.

PricewaterhouseCoopers. (2007). *Similarities and differences—a comparison of IFRS and US GAAP.* London: Author.

Securities and Exchange Commission (SEC). (2003). *Study pursuant to section 108(d) of the Sarbanes-Oxley Act of 2002 on the adoption by the US financial reporting system of a principles-based accounting system.* Washington, DC: Author.

Securities and Exchange Commission (SEC). (2005). *Report and recommendations pursuant to section 401(c) of the Sarbanes-Oxley Act of 2002 on arrangements with off-balance sheet implications, special purpose entities, and transparency of filings by issuers.* Washington, DC: Author. Retrieved from http://www.sec.gov/news/studies/soxoffbalancerpt.pdf

Soderstrom, N. S., & Sun, K. J. (2007). IFRS adoption and accounting quality: A review. *European Accounting Review, 16,* 675–702.

Tokar, M. (2005). Convergence and the implementation of a single set of global standards: The real life challenge. *Accounting in Europe, 2,* 47–68.

Walton, P. (2001, September). Tin hat time at the IASB. *Accounting & Business,* 18.

Walton, P. (2002). Henry Benson. In M. Warner (Ed.), *International encyclopedia of business and management* (2nd ed., pp. 482–486). London: Thomson Learning.

Walton, P. (2003). European harmonization. In F. D. S. Choi (Ed.), *International finance and accounting handbook* (3rd ed.). Hoboken, NJ: John Wiley & Sons.

# Index

*Note:* The italicized *f* and *t* following page numbers refer to figures and tables.